HOCKEY LEADERSHIP & COACHING

From theory to practice and drills

HockeyCoach.se – Jukka Aro

Content

A father's wish

Dear Hockey Coach,

Tomorrow my son starts to start in the hockey school. He will go out on the ice, to begin his great adventure, which I am sure will include both joy and disappointment.

I wish you could take him in the hand and teach him the things he needs to know. Teach him to respect the referee and that his judgment is final, he will not change it by complaining.

Teach him not to hate his opponents or see them as enemies, instead teach him to value them, and his own skills and performance. Teach him to compete against the situation and the challenge, not against an enemy.

Teach him to be a team player and that it each role is equally important and that the pass before a goal, is as important as it is to score. I know, the goals count, but still...

Teach him to never blame his own goalkeeper when a goal is made against him, five mistakes were made before the puck ended up in his goal.

Teach him that it is much more honorable to lose by doing his best than cheating to success.

Teach him to be a competitor who focuses on the team's goal and achievement, as well as on individual goals and his own performance.

Teach him to close his ears to unnecessary criticism from the stands and to stand up for himself in difficult situations, if he thinks he is right.
Teach him carefully, but don't curl him, because only the fire makes fine steel.

This is a great desire coach, I know, but I put my son in your hands. See what you can do for, and with him. He's such a nice little guy.

/His father

Being a leader

A leader role is not easy regardless of sport. The demands and expectations are sometimes great (you can only look at the fictional example, a father's wish). You have to deal with hockey's seasonal and training planning, create exercises, talk to parents, moms, fathers, grandparents, fans, other coaches, media, newspapers, teach ethics, be a psychologist, diplomat, win, let all players be a part of team, manage losses, have fun, coach, support, set rules, norms, visions, goals, develop team...

Or as a job ad for a youth coach could look like:

Youth Coach - Vacancy

You will work with a group of 20-30 young people. We see as a very important that you are able to motivate others, since there are different engagement levels in the group and around the team. You should create "the internal drive".

Working hours: Flexible, but usually weekday evenings, early afternoons, weekends with early mornings and full days (to some extent overnight stays are also included), even some "24/7 call service" occur, and that some tasks need of course to be handled during the day, as contacts with the employer.

Financial compensation: 0 €/$/£ (currency is not important, we look for the right candidate) You have to pay an annual membership fee of 50 €/$/£ and of course the annual fee for your own children who are part of the group or in other groups.
Pay for your profiled work clothes and other work-related personal equipment.
Pay for your trips to, and from your work (Frequent flexible travelling within the region, sometimes outside, we see it as an advantage if you have a large car).
...and participate in various events and sales activities (this is required, so you can do your work).

We view education as important and expect you to continuously educate yourself in defined training programs, to some extent at your own expense. You should also practice and participate in the trainings for: prevention of injuries, emergency care and diet counseling as well as the internal meetings (we try to schedule these as much as possible on your vacant evening so that you can participate).

You are responsible for ensuring that you, the group and relatives follow the set values and act on the basis of the developed policy, as the task is to educate future adults, by: Educating and developing all individuals in the group, starting from their conditions. (Here the requirement picture from relatives may vary and does not necessary relate to attendance and player engagement level)
Being responsible, accountable, answer and argue for your training methods, choices, results and decisions, to the group's relatives and if necessary for the employer. (Here late evening work might occur and we expect you to have your own phone)

You are responsible for ensuring that all activities are well-planned, performed efficiently, with discipline and good organization, which provides opportunities for development for everyone. This requires great flexibility and innovative ability, as the pre-conditions, training attendance, times, engagement levels etc. vary and can be changed with short notice.

You are responsible to ensure that relatives occupy a number of roles and posts around the team (you can of course have double roles) and in working groups internally and with the employer and contribute with their time and commitment according to the employer's directive.

If this sounds interesting, don't hesitate, maybe YOU'RE just the one we're looking for!?

Challenging! Still fun and developing, or otherwise no one would take such a role?
I hope that I can give you some theoretical advice and practical tools in your hockey leadership role, no, I'm pretty sure you'll find valuable tips, advice and knowledge in this book in order to be a successful and communicative leader and Hockey Coach.

The author

Who am I then? My name is Jukka Aro, born 1976 and have worked with leadership, team and operational development for almost 20 years (professionally) and as a coach on different levels for 25 years. I have the highest coaching degree of sports-specific training (ice hockey) and the highest degree for sports, from a coaching academy and other leadership and management trainings and courses. Leadership and teamwork is my profession.

Is it possible to predict success?

Is it possible to predict whether a hockey team or a leader will succeed or fail with a team? I say it is, and that luck has nothing to do with it. I will explain leadership blocks that will be used to secure your success as a hockey leader or coach. The hockey leadership model, which you will find on the following pages, can be used to build things from the beginning or to analyze where you are at the moment and which parts you can improve or you are strong in (strengths and weaknesses), the model can also be used in communication, to secure you reach out with your message.

Even though I say hockey's leadership model, it will work outside the hockey and in other sports. The leadership methods and tools are the same in football, basketball, floorball, associations, companies, boardrooms etc.

Briefly about the book before we continue

The text in the book can certainly sometimes be perceived as a bit jumpy between the headlines, because I have originally written the text in small pieces to a blog, or in some cases as short own memory notes, which create added value or I felt were important learnings.

Since the book has been written for a blog or more as a guide for leadership, it is not always like reading a "normal" book, with a clear red thread from topic to topic and between each chapter, the transitions can hang on a thin red thread in some cases, although I have spent a lot of time connecting the text.

Certain repetitions also occur when the subject can be linked to different leadership blocks depending on how the subject is angled. Your guiding light should be the different main chapters / leadership blocks where I have visualized the transitions between the blocks through the image of the leadership model and the content of the chapter is always linked to the respective leadership blocks.

I have also chosen to refer many times to football leader José Mourinho in this hockey book, although the last years have been tough for him, but I think it is important to get influences outside the "innermost hockey circle". The content is also a mixture of leadership theories, real and fictional examples, as well as practical hockey coaching from basic level to more advanced and from leadership to hockey drills.

The book should give you an overall picture of being a leader and coach both on and off the ice for your hockey team and what is required in different areas to succeed with your team. Enough with explanations and possible excuses. I am convinced that you will benefit from the book with new ideas, theories, lessons, exercises and to structure your previous skills to develop yourself as a leader and your team.

When it comes to the grammatical and language in the book, I'm Finnish (mother tongue), living in Sweden and fluent in Swedish, so English is my third language, if you find some grammatical errors or funny / strange expression, you know why... Please try to see above the "Swenglish" and just try to catch the message ☺

The leadership model

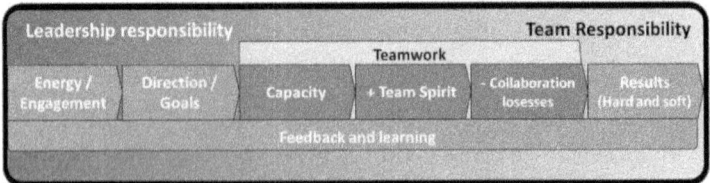

About the leadership model

Above you see my interpretation of what needs to be in place to succeed as a leader of a team or a working group. I have combined some different leadership models and theories into one own coherent leadership model, these are the elements that I think you need to work on getting in place in each team to be successful.

I see a clear connection between a group's success and how well you get the different blocks in place. So in other words, success is predictable, and luck has nothing to do with lasting success!

The first part that must be in place is energy / engagement. When you have energy / engagement, you have to steer and direct it. When you have energy / engagement and direction, you have to get the team to work together (Teamwork) this part consists of three important components, capacity, team spirit and collaborative losses.

When the first three blocks are in place, you can expect results and these can vary depending on how you succeeded with the first three blocks. You must take care of the results

14

that comes from the process within the team and visualize those and communicate these.

The last part is about feedback, feedback can be given on each individual block and will strengthen the different blocks in the management model, depending on how the feedback is given.

I will now begin to explain each block more in detail, but still at the overall level to give you the whole picture before we go into details, theories, methods and tools and deep dives into each block.

*"We lead the league with nine points. Is it because we have
been lucky? Of course not. It is about anything but luck when
you talk about my players."*
/ José Mourinho

Leadership responsibility vs Team responsibility

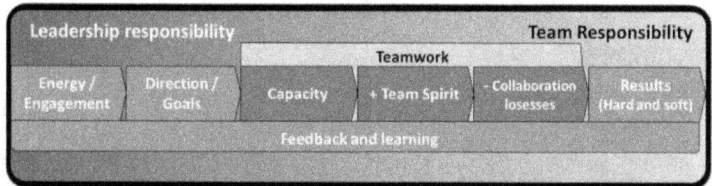

The scale

At the top you can see a scale describing the split of responsibility between the leader and the team, it's not a sharp line, but leadership responsibility is more to the left and team responsibility from middle towards the right.

Of course, the leader is always responsible for all aspects and especially for the team's results and performance, but it is the team that delivers the results and makes the work. The leader's main elements are at the beginning, with the creation of energy / engagement, focus the energy through the formulation of goals and strengthening the teamwork block.

The team's main responsibility is the team work as such (performance) and results, with obvious support and guidance from the leader.

Feedback is a shared responsibility, from coach to team, from team member to team member and from player to coach.

Energy / Engagement

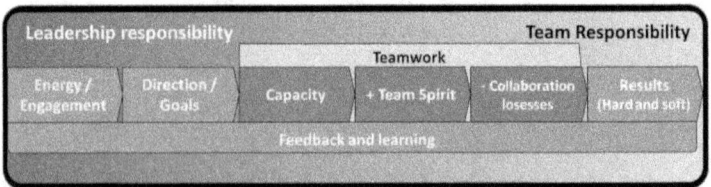

Energy / Engagement

To explain why we do something or why we need to do things in a certain way is the foundation of energy, together with the description of opportunities, obstacles and threats.

If you do not know why or do something because you "must" without understanding why, you will never have any extra engagement and energy to do so, because you do not understand why, and it can only feel unnecessary when there is a lack of understanding.

You as a leader or coach also need to know the reason why your players are there. Why are they in the team and why do they come to the training? What drives the individual player? This will help you understand the individual driving force of each player when you know why they are there.

"Here, in every exercise, every match and every minute of your social life must steer towards the goal of being a champion"
"First line" will not be a correct word. I need you all. You need each other. We are one team." (In a letter sent to the players)
/ José Mourinho

Goals / Direction

Leadership responsibility					Team Responsibility
			Teamwork		
Energy / Engagement	Direction / Goals	Capacity	+ Team Spirit	- Collaboration losesses	Results (Hard and soft)
		Feedback and learning			

Goals / Direction

When energy / engagement is there by understanding why, why we are there, why we practice in a certain way, why we practice different things etc. We need to control the energy / engagement with what we strive for, what is the purpose, what is the goal for the drill / practice, what is our vision, goals, focus areas, norms, rules, values etc.

The vision, goals and objectives guide the achievement in the desired direction, norms, values and rules will indicate the direction for team work within the team. You have a limited amount of energy, steer it against what you want to achieve or improve. What is the goal and purpose, with what we do?

"I want to see Mr. Moratti holding the trophy and watching him cry."

"I have to defend what is mine. Currently, it's my Champions League. I'm the last winner - so it's my tournament."

"I'm absolutely sure we'll be champions next season."
/ José Mourinho

Teamwork

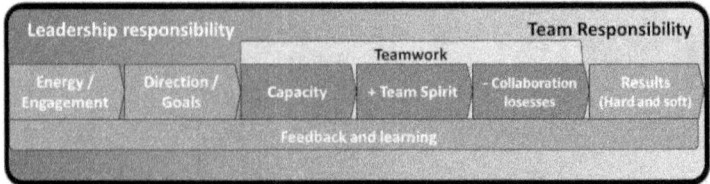

Teamwork

Teamwork = (Capacity + team spirit) - Collaboration losses
The third block is about teamwork, how you and your players work together.
The three parts in the middle are about teamwork within the team during a training, match and outside, the parts come from Steiner's model with small changes, it describes the group's cooperation and the conditions for achieving results. The Steiner model is based on what we can strengthen within our team, capacity and team spirit and try to minimize the third, collaborative losses.

Capacity can be defined e.g. such as training and utilization of knowledge, skills, physical, mental skills, equipment, facilities, coaches, training times and opportunities etc.

Team spirit can sometimes be difficult to define, it is something that is in the group and that makes the team stronger. Togetherness, clear roles, security, appreciation, positive climate, community, common vision and goals can be some keywords when we talk about team spirit, 1 + 1 becomes more than two.

Collaboration losses can involve, for example, unclear roles, incorrect positions on the plan, bad passes, unsynchronized activities, bad timing, in short, all "errors" that complicate and impair the team.

The second part of collaborative losses is about loss of motivation in groups.

Motivation losses tend to occur when the team size increases, or when the leader does not see all the players, then you suddenly do not get 100% from each team member, this phenomenon is called social loafing, the player / players feel that "I am not important for the team and I don't have to do my best, my achievement is not so important and will not be visible, to the team, the leader or the audience."

"We have top-class players and, sorry if I sound arrogant, we have a top-class trainer" / José Mourinho

Results

Results

What have we achieved? What results can you see? It is important to see both hard (objective) results, such as points, improved speed (time), skills (skills track on time) etc. But also to see the soft results, such as improved cooperation / teamwork, team spirit, communication, fighting spirit etc. The follow-up of the results is usually a minor problem in sport, than in, for example, many workplaces.

In sports you have the points in the match, your league position, how many goals you have done, how many goals you have allowed, power play statistics, number of shots etc. but in the workplace it can be more diffuse many times, how do you know you are doing a good job, or how do you know you are performing at work? Many companies strive for "world class", but have not defined it, or have no idea what it really means, or how their competitors perform, there is no league table available and updated weekly.
Visualize what you have achieved, hard and soft results. Small and large. Short and long term. Visualization of results will also strengthen the "direction" of energy.

"We're not entertaining? Okay, I don't care, we win ..." / José Mourinho

Feedback

Leadership responsibility					Team Responsibility
			Teamwork		
Energy / Engagement	Direction / Goals	Capacity	+ Team Spirit	- Collaboration losesses	Results (Hard and soft)
Feedback and learning					

Feedback

How was the result? How was the energy, motivation, teamwork and results? What did we do well? What can be improved? What have we learned? What do we take with us in the future? Your feedback will affect all parts of the model, energy, direction, cooperation and the results you will achieve in the future, or specific depending on your approach, where do you want a changed behavior or what behavior do you want to keep and strengthen?

This is perhaps the part that many of us do not spend so much time on, or if we lack time, e.g. after a practice, this is the block we are likely to skip, but this is an important part. It is about learning for the future, for the next exercise, training, match, so that we will be improving our performance over time.

"We should have won this game with seven players. Perhaps with sex we would have had to fight, but we would have won with seven." / José Mourinho

"I hate to talk to players individually. Players do not win trophies, teams win trophies ... I love players who love to win. / José Mourinho

Categorize your previous knowledge

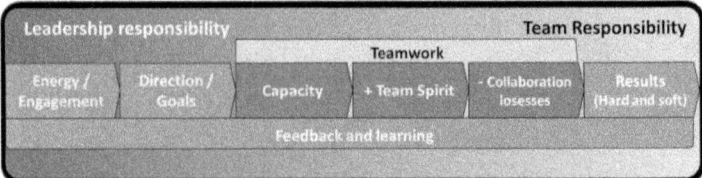

Categorize your previous knowledge

You probably already have a good and broad knowledge of many of the blocks, this is a good way to structure the previous knowledge, at least it is so for me.

Many times you participate in special courses and training on goal setting, collaboration or team building, but you get no holistic view or how the parts are connected, affect and interlink with each other. I think this model can give you the links and a way to structure it.

Jose Mourinho quotes are in some cases "over the border" or even extreme and therefore you have to find your own way of expressing things, but I believe his statements clearly visualize e.g. his goal for the next season and what he wants with the team.

With his clear communication, the goals or the type of rules and norms he has and values within the team become clear to all players involved, the people around the team, including the media and the fans.

Analyze your team's strengths, weaknesses, opportunities and threats – SWOT

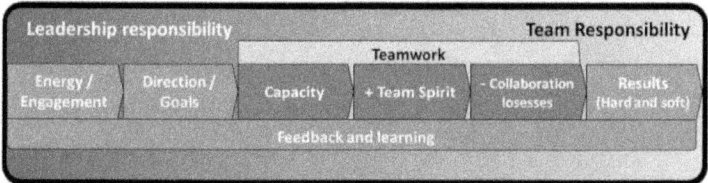

Analyze your team's strengths, weaknesses, opportunities and threats – SWOT (Strengths, Weaknesses, Opportunities and Threats)

Use the blocks to analyze your own team, where you are strong and where are you weak. You can use the model at different levels, for the whole organization, the club, for the team, the group of players, e.g. goalkeepers, defense, or forwards and for individual players and of course for yourself as a coach.

It is also suitable for the whole season, every practice or for each drill. Why do we have this drill? What is the purpose of it, what do want to improve? What / Who Do You Need to perform it? What are the teaching points (to avoid co-operational losses)? How was the result? What could you see? How did the players feel that they were performing? What worked well? What can be improved?

Or from a team perspective, why are we in this team, what's the purpose of what we are doing? What is our purpose, what are we aiming for? How should we do it? Where or how can we see the results? How can we learn during the journey? This activity can of course and should be in different dimensions, short-, mid- and long-term.

In the beginning I also mentioned the model can be used for communication. When you are delivering a message or speech, why are you doing it, what do you want to achieve with you message, what does the audience need to know-feel-do? How will you do it, just talk, use a flipchart, PowerPoint? How do you know you get the results with the communication (look back to the three words, know – feel – do), finally ask for feedback, what was good, what can improved?

This is the model in brief at the overall level and we will now start to dig into each part deeper, I personally think it is better to give you the overall picture at a high level before we go into the details, so you don't have to try to figure out how the picture of this puzzle looks when you read the details and that at the end you understand how everything is connected.

I think you already now have a pretty good picture of the message I want to convey? Now we will only strengthen each part more theoretically, practically and with more details.

Before you continue reading

It was the introduction at the overall level, I hope you have an overview and understanding of the management model and the blocks and parts on which it is based.

"The text in the book can certainly sometimes be perceived as something jumpy between the headlines, it is because I have originally written the text in small pieces to a blog, or in some cases as short own memory notes, which create added value. Since it has been written for a blog or more as a guide for leadership, it is not always like reading a "normal" book, with a clear red thread from topic to topic and between each chapter, the transitions can hang on a thin red thread in some cases, although I have spent a lot of time connecting the text Certain repetitions also occur when the subject can be linked to different leadership blocks depending on how the subject is angled. Your guiding light may be the different chapters / leadership blocks where I have visualized the transitions between the blocks through the image of the leadership model and the content of the chapter is always linked to the respective leadership blocks.
I have also chosen to refer many times to football leader José Mourinho in this hockey book, as I think it is important to get influences outside the "innermost circle".
The content is also a mixture of leadership theories, real and fictional examples, as well as practical hockey coaching from basic level to more advanced and from leadership to hockey exercises.
The book should give you an overall picture of being a leader and coach both on and off the ice for your hockey team and what is required in different areas to succeed with your team.

Enough with explanations and possible excuses. I am convinced that you will benefit from the book with new ideas, theories, lessons, exercises and to structure your previous skills to develop yourself as a leader and your team. "

"Repetition is a powerful teaching method and tool. Through repetition, an idea will be integrated as a normal thing, even though it was innovative or completely new from the beginning."

Energy / Engagement

Leadership responsibility		Teamwork			Team Responsibility
Energy / Engagement	Direction / Goals	Capacity	+ Team Spirit	- Collaboration losesses	Results (Hard and soft)
Feedback and learning					

Energy / Engagement

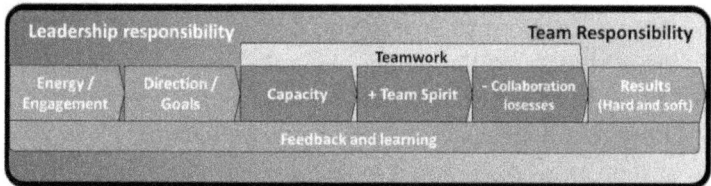

Category: Energy / Engagement: Explaining why we do something or why we do things in a certain way is the foundation together with the description of opportunities and threats. If you do not know why you are doing or should do something, you will never have any extra motivation to do so, because you do not understand the why.

The power in three letters
Think of a situation where you did not have the true energy or motivation to do something. A situation where you couldn't feel any desire to do it at all. Do you have the picture and the feeling, for that situation?

Was there something missing or something said or why didn't you feel motivated? Was the task important to you, or to someone else?

I can use one of my examples, it is of course from the sport. I played hockey and had my position on the right side. On some of the exercises on our hockey training I would go up the red line and then turn and go towards the middle, and then the defender would pass the puck on the same side that I went from, to another forward.

I found it totally unnecessary and worthless to do so and therefore asked the coach why I would go as I did, I got the answer that I needed to do it, it was part of the exercise... How do you think an 11-12 year old feels for such a hockey drill? Hardly exciting, motivating or energizing? It certainly did not energize me, because at that moment I did not understand why I did it and it looked like my coach did not understand either, that was how the exercise should be, point, just skate! Then you can quickly reflect on the model and connect to both the energy block, but also the cooperation losses, unless the players understand why they should go certain paths, they most likely do not have good timing in the skating either.

When we are still on the theme, my view is that the players should rather be asked for problem solving, than ready-made tracks, because how often does everything that you have drawn up on a paper go that way in a game? Then it is good with some own understanding of the game, of course some basics must always be there. In this case the problem is a 2 against 1 situation in the neutral zone, how do we get into the offensive zone, cooperating, using our resources and the 2 – 1 advantage?

Explain why

What if the coach would have explained it in the following way? You have to go along the board, then turn in at the red line (then there was still red line offside), to get the left defenseman to follow you into the middle, by doing this you create space at the board for your line mate, just because their defensive player follows you to the middle and therefore we can pass the puck to our other forward in the space you have created through your skating and from there we can start our next move, you make an important move, to create space and time for your teammate and for us to continue our attack, and if their defenseman does not follow you, you are the one who gets the pass during the match.

So what was the secret? The explanation of why you are doing something, the importance of the activity, linked to understanding the obstacles / threats and opportunities. Can you see the difference in motivation and energy level of a young player?

Mourinho, does he need to explain why?

Of course, José Mourinho does not face this simple problem, but he still has to explain why, many, many times to his players. Sometimes it is even harder to get your experienced players to try to do some new things, because some of them will be "well, but we are used to do things this way", and then you really have to explain why they need to do things different or your way.

Here are some of the "lacy" explanations, why things can't be done.

- "Yes, but we are different"

- "Yes, but we have already tried it before"

- "Yes, but our players don't like it"

- "Yes, but my responsibility will change"

- "Yes, but it will destroy our game"

- "Yes, but it does not fit our structure"

- "Yes, but our fans don't need it"

- "Yes, but we are obliged to ..."

Thank you to the "Why not players"!

Yes, but will stop a lot of development and drive in your team and sometimes it's good to ask the question back, why not? This question will many times open up the thinking, is there a strong reasoning behind, or maybe it will be obvious for the one receiving the question back that it could be worth trying.

Understanding why is also important in other contexts, why do you play hockey, why are you in this hockey team, why do you come to the hockey training, what is your driving force?

You can also ask that question for yourself, why do you coach, why are you a hockey coach? What are your motives and driving forces for your leadership, why are you a leader?

Below some generic why-reasons for playing hockey.

Non-professional hockey players (main reasons)
Really Young Hockey Player: Why are you playing?

- I want to be a hockey pro

- My parents want me to play

- I have my best friend Charlie here

- It's fun (the follow-up question should be, why do you feel it's fun?)

Junior Hockey player: Why are you playing?

- I want to be a hockey pro or at least try to make some money on it

- I have my friends here

- I like hockey (the follow-up question should be, why do you like hockey?)

I think the second category from really young hockey players (my parents want me to play) gives a signal that these players will disappear if that's the only reason to play hockey, because my parents want, that will not last long term as the reason for that, of course these players can find a new why reason during the journey, but might need some support.

Half-professional hockey players: why do you play?

- I get some extra money

- I like the talk in the locker room

- I just like it, its part of me

- It keeps me in shape

- It's nice to say I'm a hockey player, to the girls in the bar

- I like hockey

- I still have a dream of playing higher up in the series system

Professional hockey players (main reasons)

- I earn my living

- I want to win the league / big titles

- I want to be a better hockey player

- I like the talk in the locker room

- I just like it, its part of me

- I like hockey

- I want to win (matches, series, and tournaments)

- That's the only thing I can and know

Look at each group and you can find better or less good "why reasons" and statements to play hockey.

"I told Adrian Mutu, you are already a rich boy, you make a lot of money, you still have a big contract. So no problem with your future in terms of money, no problems with prestige in your home country. When you go back to Romania you will be one of the kings, but five years after you left the football no one will remember you, only if you do big things. You are here to create history "/ José Mourinho

When you practice hockey at "lower" levels, you need to understand why your players are there, in order to pull the right strings, how does it look in your team? Will your hockey players have many different reasons why they play hockey, have you asked them? What are their driving forces? Many times it is good to have several reasons, in order to have the motivation overtime to continue playing, if the only reason is to, let's say win games, this could be a big pitfall in the long run, if it's supported by other reasons like, I have my best friends here, the probability for that player to continue to play hockey over time increases.

You may need to adjust your expectations and requirements for players at lower levels, or you may get good reason not to take them into the squad with this dialogue. Perhaps you should choose the player who wants to develop, before a "medium good" player who only uses hockey as a status symbol e.g. in the bar, although the first player would not be as good as the others (this is a real practical example if it looks and sounds strange to you)

Why are your players there?

What if you are a coach for a professional hockey team? Somehow there is no difference, you still need to know why, why are your players there, the main reason is not only that they have a contract with the team (in that case they are probably already on the bench) or that they want to earn a lot money, because they already have it. So what is it then?

It's a question I can't give you the right answer to, you need to know your players to understand the driving force, why they continue their career and what motivates them, and I mean each one of them, because you won't get the same answer from each of the players!

In connection with the above and next part "closest to the heart" it may be good to get a picture of how our personality is structured. The following is a general model for describing personality.

What creates personality in hockey?

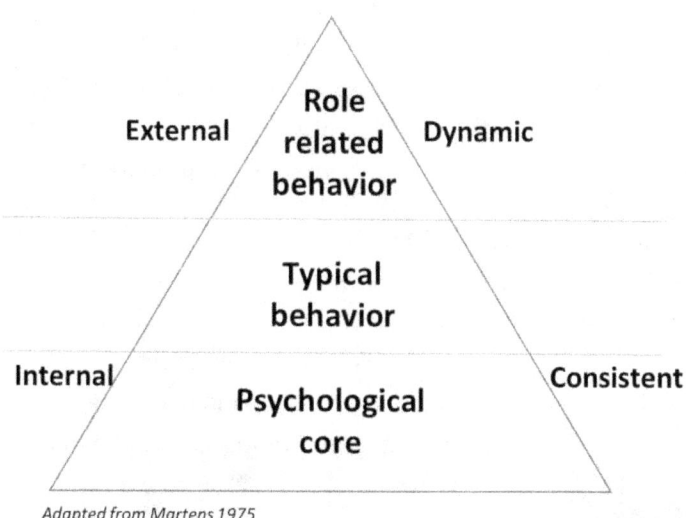

External — Role related behavior — Dynamic

Typical behavior

Internal — Psychological core — Consistent

Adapted from Martens 1975

Psychological core - The deepest component in creating our personality includes our values, attitudes, interests and motives (what will create genuine inner motivation and energy, what matters to us and is rooted within us). This is "the real you", this part also contains our belief in ourselves and self-confidence.

Typical behaviors - How we adapt to the environment, or how we will probably react in different situations, excited, energetic, tired, not interested, happy, shy, open, want to be at the center of attention etc. Sometimes people can be wrongly judged on their typical behaviors, if you only see one person once or the first time in a team and that person is currently "tired", he / she is simply placed in the "tired /

39

uninterested" box but it can only be the current situation or the night before, which created the typical "tired" behavior, that is not the way this person usually works. Or that someone is silent and observes at some point or more often than others, does not necessary mean that that person is introvert, it could be the typical situation adapted behavior.

Role-Related Behavior - This behavior is the most changing aspect of our personality. Different situations require different roles, actions and behavior. During the day you can switch between some of these roles, hockey coach, dad / mom, husband / wife, employee, friend, and of course you will show different levels of energy / motivation and behavior for a task.

Knowing your hockey players will help you in your coaching role and in your way to coach the team and the individuals. You know the basics of how your players are and will probably work and act in different situations.

Knowing your players well and deeply also helps you understand their "drive", what drives them, and makes them perform at their peak.

Motives and motives can still change over time, so you must continue to follow up and understand why your players are there to be able to motivate them in the right way, even in the future, so in other words it is no "one timer" rather a "rebound".

There is a statement that is, the deeper your relationships are, the stronger your leadership is. True? I don't have the right answer, but if you look at José Mourinho it may be true.

http://youtu.be/nUD4IxLIPuo

Materazzi might not be a player in the "first line", but this video shows how valued and important he was for Mourinho and the team, although he often sat on the bench. (Video from Mourinho leaving Inter for Madrid and the good bye with Materazzi)

If you study José Mourinho's leadership and relationship with the players, it is sometimes described as father-son relationship, or that he is a big brother the players look up to. If you have that kind of close relationship, he certainly knows his players pretty well and what motivates them in different situations.

Of course you can feel your players well without having a father-son relationship, and it will work well!

"Compared to Rafa Benitez, Mourinho had a close relationship with the players and was more open and humorous" / Javier Zanetti (FC Inter Captain)

For me, the team or why do I do it?

If we continue with what motivates us, there is a general model, to talk about individual motivation. The closer things are to your "heart" or the psychological core, the more it will motivate you (internal motivation), or in other words, give you more energy to perform, train and activate you.

To create your own drive for the training

 One area that should put a lot of effort into is to get your own drive for the training. Today, many or more precisely, all young people have a simple alternative in their pocket or at home, which easily precedes both homework and training...

As a coach you can drive the process to create your own drive, but we can never be a players "own drive / engagement". One way to create insight both for you as the coach and the player is to talk about what drives or creates motivation for each individual player.

Part one is to understand why? Why does the player come to the training? Why does he think it's fun? Why, why why...

Motivation in the Stone Age

To really understand what's already built inside us, we have to move back in time. Really to the first people on earth, what was their motivation and drive?

In order to survive, they needed food, if you didn't find any food your own body = you would suffer, in the next step the motivation for helping your own family and after that your relatives, other families and perhaps "friends" would drive and engage your hunting. It was basic, but once you have achieved that, you could get extra attention by being the best hunter (your professional role) and you could get a better position in the "team" thanks to it.

If you were really good at what you did, your reputation could also spread to other villages and communities.

It can be easy to make connections from many parts in the history to today's hockey or society with likes, status updates etc. but it is far back in time and I'm not a historian teacher, but it sounds as a logical connection?

Motivation in modern times

If we translate it to modern times, can it be that the same basics still exist? If your own body is threatened or if you see an opportunity that benefits you, you will react, you will be motivated to do things, right?

You will try to run / "fight" or take the opportunity, because it is about you, you are the most important, for you! Things that affect you will always create energy and motivation to do things to get something, or to avoid some bad things happening.

Newspaper Headlines!

Think of the headlines or the flyers for the different newspapers or news articles on the web, each heading is formulated so that you have to react and buy the newspaper, or click on the link on the website. "Top 50 People that Earned most money in Your City", "The New ... Read How You Will Be Affected", "Ketchup Causes Cancer, You Can be Affected", "Want to get in shape, we have the 5 min workout for you"

If you don't buy the magazine or click the link to visit the site, the creators of the headlines have failed ... Since the only purpose of the headings and the first pages is to create a feeling (a possibility or a potential threat)! You have something to gain, lose, you will be affected or be interested, because it can touch you (near the heart), so you will buy the newspaper, magazine or click into the website.

José Mourinho reveals his leadership secrets! Get your hockey team to perform on top! 10 Easy Practical Steps!

Would you buy the book or the newspaper? 10 simple steps! Sounds interesting, however it is not usually the secret, it is required a little more than that, but often it causes us to react and act (here is an opportunity and maybe a short cut to success).

How can you, as a coach, think a little more like a "headline designer" and get your players interested in buying your ideas with a high motivation to also perform these practically?

Awaken the interest and connect this to your players. What's in it for them?

Players on the transfer list

Players who are on the transfer list or are hit by rumors of "changing team" will in many cases perform outstanding (new opportunity, contract with new club or improved negotiating position with current, but sometimes these players will perform poorly because they are too affected by this and choose to "escape" or "run away (become passive)" from the situation. In any case, the situation has created energy, but as in the other case, it was wrongly directed (escape).

These situations you will face many times, even if it's not about changing a team. Some players will step up ready for a challenge while others will "hide" and try to "escape", the only tool for you as a coach, that can help in this situation is to have a dialogue and understand the reasons for the reaction and after that practice these situations in different formats.

What we care about will motivate us

The things that are closest to each individual's heart will create energy / motivation to do something, it will differ between people, but below you will find some general things that motivate people and your players, things that make people react to something in way or other, if there is a threat or opportunity.

You need to find out this image for each of your players in order to motivate them, by understanding their closest to "heart" things related to hockey. The closer the things are to you or your "ego/heart", the more reaction it will create, the order may vary between people and there are of course many other things to put in there, but here is a general model that makes us react and are prepared to act on opportunities or threats.

If something favors or threatens any of the following categories, a reaction, motivation to "escape or fight" is created.

Test yourself. **You are criticized for your...** *try the sentences from 1 to 6.* **Is there a reaction for you?** Would you be ready to act?

1. Your own body / You

2. Family, relatives and friends (teammates, here or later, depending on team spirit)

3. Properties and talents

4. Opinions and values

5. Social status, professional role, performance, possessions, appearance etc.

6. Club, nation, culture etc.

...or do it in a more positive way: Use the sentences
1 to 6.. ...will get an "opportunity", if you train / take care / change / improve.

This is a general picture and which I wrote earlier and it can vary a lot between people or in this case team members in which priority order these are located. How did you feel about the test for yourself?

Was there areas where you would be less like to react or do things?

Why do you do things, what are the motives?

What do you think of your hockey training, why do your players come there? What are their motives or their "nearest heart things"? Some of the answers you have already read about, but you have to explore this more in your own team, to understand your players and to be able to pull the right strings. Why should they always get there from an individual perspective, reminding them of their own driving force.

http://youtu.be/_ZpDnXYIFjo

See the first 15 seconds, to get the explanation why Waterboy chose the special course at school, where he is part of the school's American football team.

The cause may not be something that the teacher was aware of? How do you motivate a student / player as "waterboy"?

... and the most interesting, I managed to create a sentence that aroused your curiosity, which made you type the link in your mobile / computer or clicked the link in the electronic version? (Reaction = energy, activity = direction, click on the link)

What motivates a hockey coach?

What then motivates a hockey coach or what motivates a coach like José Mourinho? What motivates you, is it clear to yourself? What are the things that will give you extra energy or energy to act?

We will always come into periods when the motivation is not at the top and then it helps to have a clear picture of what is important and a driving force for you, it helps you past the heavier periods or through the good ones with even greater driving force.

After winning the triple with Inter, José Mourinho declared immediately after, his work was done. He had created history with the team and he needed new challenges in a new team (Real Madrid).

I think José Mourinho finds his motivation and energy in striving for the big titles, creating history and building underdog teams to champions (it is perhaps difficult to say that Real Madrid is underdogs, but at this time they were).

- Porto had a hard time, Mourinho made them the Champions League winners

- Chelsea had not won the Premier League for 50 years, before Mourinho came, after winning the Premier League twice and four cup titles.

- Inter struggled in the Champions League, the last victory was in 1965. With Mourinho's lead, they won Serie A, Copa Italia and the Champions League in the same season.

- Real Madrid has won the UEFA Champions League 2002 and La Liga 2008, so it has been a while since the last victory, for a team of Real Madrid caliber, that's why Mourinho went to Madrid, this is his challenge and motivation to get back the big titles to Madrid and himself manage to lead teams to titles in different leagues and win the Champions League with and by building different teams to strong and competitive units.

By explaining why and finding topics that are important to each person, you can motivate others. What you do by that is to make them take a "step across the line" from passive to active members, picking up their own drive to succeed.

When you succeed, you can expect really good results, both soft and hard, for the individual, as for the team. Your own drive needs to be and can be attracted by you as a leader by, creating understanding of why, with connection to what the player thinks is important for himself.

A practical example – Penalty shot or Shootout

Let's take an example of why we do things or choose not to. Penalty shot or a shootout. Think about the reactions this situation will create among your players. How many of them would cross the line to face the challenge? How many would like to disappear from the bench? Why would they do that?

If you hadn't pointed out a shooter, what reactions would this situation create inside your players?

Most of them would see this as a threatening situation (they are personally affected) and would do everything possible to avoid the situation (excuses, refer to fatigue, minor injuries, lack of training, and shift responsibility between the team members you can take, then you, etc.) Why would your players want to take the penalty shot (step over the line)?

1. Your own body / You

2. Family, relatives and friends (teammates, here or further away)

3. Properties and talents

4. Opinions and values

5. Social status, professional role, performance, possessions, appearance etc.

6. Club, nation, culture etc.

Selfish reasons, I want to be in focus (1.). I do it for the team and my teammates (2.). I get an opportunity to expand the professional role (I also get the chance next time) (5.). I do it for my nation, I want to be the national hero (selfish reason?) (6.)

The players who find these why reasons inside them will probably be more successful than a player who is forced to take the penalty shot, they may just ask themselves, WHY ME?

Therefore, it is also important to work on visualizing the possibilities and try to eliminate or at least minimize the threat picture that the player feels through dialogue (if it's a shootout in a normal game, "we already have one point, one more is just a bonus"), but also facts (coming later in the book). Communication and dialogue is the key in this situation.

The answer to why, on the training

Other areas to think about with the why explanation is when choosing drills for your training, why this one? / Why these drills / exercises? Once you have the answer yourself, you are able to explain the why part to your players also when explaining the drills, not just the how to do part, and with that visualizing the purpose and creating engagement, this is an important drill/practice for us because of... The explanation could be something like on the next page...

1. Why 2. What 3. How

The next exercise "*Name that explain the exercise*" (think of the title or the headliner for the newspapers), we do it "*why / purpose explanation*" and we will do it like this "*practical how the explanation with technical / tactical teaching and focus points*".

If you manage to explain why and find topics that are important to each person, motivate others, you will get them to "step across the line" (get involved). This will appear in:

- All team members are personally involved and interested in the team's success

- All players understand why they are in the team (their role) and what impact they have on the whole team's performance and results.

When communicating continuously why and trying to connect it to each of the players "closest to the heart". (The team's success should be a common interest for each player)

... and therefore everyone realizes that their contribution will make a difference to the team and themselves, from forwards to goalkeeper!

For me or for someone else?

So far I have mixed internal and external motivation, but what is best and what is the difference between internal and external motivation?

Internal or external motivation?

The internal motivation comes from you, you do something because you want (and you know why) and you can see the benefits for you and it triggers you. External motivation comes from external rewards, such as prices, money or other benefits and creates a driving force for you.

It can be difficult to say what motivated you the most, but in the long run, the internal motivation (your own drive) is the motivation that will help you most in your performance. Other sources of motivation may be:

- Task-related motivation, comes from the goal and purpose of the team, common efforts towards a common goal.

- Socially related motivation comes from the relationship and co-operation with the other team members

What is the individually most important factor for success?

Your own drive and your own will to develop! After that, the coach's, leaders 'and parents' real interest in the sport and to meet the players from their starting point, the next step in the development is not being a NHL star, there will be some intermediate goals along the way...

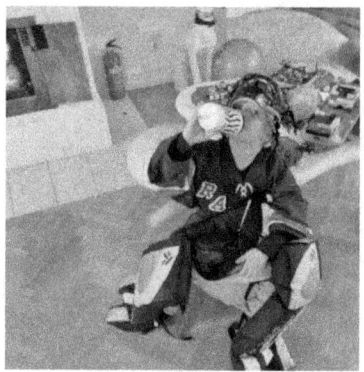 While it is very good with driven people around the team, it is important as a leader and coach to keep an eye on the different wills. The parents are key persons and if they lack the true will/purpose, it also affects the players and can be the "tongue on the wave" for a continuation of the hockey. The children are very much mirrored by their parents' level of interest. Therefore, be an interested and committed role model, as a leader, coach or parent! Finnish hockey uses three words for parents, support, drive (car) and pay.

Rewards can increase motivation?

Will you be motivated by rewards and money? Yes, most people probably answer without thinking. So here's a little story:

There was a group of boys who used to play football on a field that a farmer owned. The farmer himself did not like this and tried repeatedly to drive away the small football players, without success.

Therefore, he decided to change tactics. He went up to the boys who played football and said that everyone would get $ 5, every time they played football at his field. The week after he praised them and gave them $ 10 each.

The week after, he told the boys that he lacked money so they could only get $ 5 again. The following week he said that he could only pay $ 1. The young footballers were really upset, "Who do you think you are? How can you believe any of us would play for you, for $ 1?

What the boys had done with joy and because it was fun (inner motivation) ended as the farmer wanted, they stopped playing when the external reward was first added, raised, minimized and taken away and the original motivation was forgotten...

This can be a problem in many youth teams, when the parents pay money to their child when he / she scores goals. In this case, it will affect both your own motivational part and your teamwork. If there are no goals made, the performance feels like a big failure and if it is repeated in the next match you can think of the feeling. Your performance is only measured in number of goals and you get your money from that, little bit too tough situation for young children.

A 6-13 year old player is not prepared to let anyone else make a goal if they can earn $ 5-10 by doing it themselves (I have used the hockey movie The Pee-Wee to discuss many of the norm discussions, this is one of the topics in the movie). Paying money for goals will be seen in desperate shots from all locations and angles, even if a team mate would be free. Here it is time to give feedback and create norms and rules for the parents around the team. Is it OK to pay for individual goals, when we talk about team sports, even if it is the goals that count and most goals win? If you do not think this is OK, be clear with the why reason, why you do not want the parents to pay for goals and what you strive for as a team, when you talk to the parent / parents.

What you should pay attention to afterwards is what happens and what reactions in behavior you can see in the player(s) if the $ 5-10 is removed for each goal the player scores, if that has been the case, will hockey still be fun and will the young hockey player continue his "career"? Or to make a follow up, has the payments ended, or is it just a naive belief from your side?

Here it is important that you as a leader work with returning to the basics with the player, why is hockey really fun, what others driver does he have and working with feedback in other areas than just goal scoring towards the players.

Other examples of external motivation

When a man comes home with flowers, the question can be "Okay, what have you done now, why do you come home with flowers"? Or when you get or are offered something for free, you immediately think "What do they want me to buy from them or what type of subscription / contract lies behind the gift, what do I tie up on? "(Right thought many times ;-)

Rewards are good and fun, but you have to understand that people or your players perceive it very differently. If you give something, it is therefore good to explain and justify why you give the player / person something, not to lose the right effect.

Otherwise, some people get the feeling that the other person is trying to take control of me and tie me up by giving me something or it will negatively affect the motivation and cooperation within the team in the long term (as in the example before).

"It's good to have money, so you can buy things that can be bought with money. However, it is much better not to lose the things that cannot be bought with money = It is better to have internal than external motivation"

Motivation to stay in the team

As far as motivation is concerned, we have so far talked about explaining why, find the closest to "heart things" for each player, and to understand the motivation both internal and external motivation of your players.

So what does it look like when we talk about the motivation to continue or stay in the same team? A quite hot and valid topic in today's society, where 13-14 year olds can in some cases have played in 3-8 different teams already, where the "distance" between the teams, so to speak, allows it.

Motivation to stay in the team can be divided into two categories:

- Forces that attract team members to the team. The forces that will attract will be task-oriented, to win matches, tournaments and titles to achieve success, both as team and individually.

- Resistance to fragmentation (forces within the team to continue as teams). We are a team. We have fought together, one for all and all for one!

Zlatan Ibrahimovic left Inter for Barcelona to win the Champions League (Forces that attract team members to the team).

Inter with Jose Mourinho won Serie A, Copa Italia and the Champions League, the year when Ibrahimovic left...

Mourinho left Inter for Real Madrid (Forces that attract team members to the team), but most of the inter-players stayed in the team (opposition to split up), although there were many rumors of transitions, but not many of them proved true when it came to crunch. The power to stay in the same team was stronger than the attraction of other teams.

Turnover among hockey players and employees

Research shows that a high turnover among players / employees is expensive, (how much research is really required to come to that conclusion?) The staff / player turnover is also time consuming and adversely affects the satisfaction and communication among the players in the team (team spirit and cooperation losses).

When it comes to changing coaches, it looks as if the change is basically only linked to negative results when changing coaches (or outgoing contracts). The first immediate effect of a new voice can be positive, but it is not guaranteed and the next change in a short time may have a negative effect.

"The magic triple we won with Mourinho, no one can remove from us, and we have the same team as last year, so no one can say we can't do it again" / Javier Zanetti

Goals / Direction

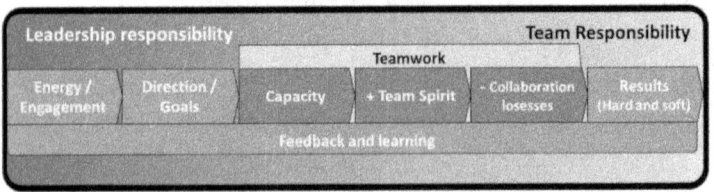

Goals / Direction and Goal setting

Leadership responsibility					Team Responsibility	
			Teamwork			
Energy / Engagement	Direction / Goals	Capacity	+ Team Spirit	- Collaboration lossess	Results (Hard and soft)	
Feedback and learning						

Category: Goals / Direction and Goal setting

When energy / motivation is there by we understand why, why we are there, why we train in a certain way, why we train different things etc. So we need to control the energy / engagement with what we strive for, what is the purpose, what is our vision, goals, goals, focus areas, action plans, norms, rules etc.

The vision, goals and goals guide the achievement in the desired direction, norms and rules will indicate the direction for teamwork within the team. You have a limited amount of energy, control it against what you want to achieve or improve. What is the goal and purpose, with what we do, both soft and hard?

"I want to see Mr. Moratti holding the trophy and watching him cry." / José Mourinho

"I have to defend what is mine. Currently, it's my Champions League. I'm the last winner - so it's my tournament." "I'm absolutely sure we'll be champions next season." / José Mourinho

If the first step or block was about the power of why, then this block is about WHAT, what is the goal, the direction, the vision, quite simply what is the purpose, what are we striving for, how do we target the energy we have created? WHAT are we aiming for?

Once you have created energy, you need to target it. It can be done in many different ways, I will give you some examples in different ways. You can do it on a vision level, then pointing the direction at least 2-3 years away, or sometimes longer. The next level is long-term goals 1-2 years away, and the short-term goals can vary from what is the goal of a hockey training or exercise, to goals for the coming months (1-12 months or sub-season goals).

In addition to the goals, you can also talk about focused areas to achieve the goals, that at the moment something of the following is important e.g. puck control, rapid attacks, strength, speed, number of shots on target per individual / team, blocked shots etc. This will also target the energy within the hockey team against what behavior you want to achieve and see an improvement within.

An interesting survey done in some major companies' shows the following: (these are real figures)

37% of employees have a clear understanding of what the organization is trying to achieve (the goals)

20% of the employees were enthusiastic about the team / organization's goals

20% of employees were able to see the connection between their own team and the organizational goals

15% of the employees believe that they can contribute towards the goals

20% of employees trust the organization they work for

Right interesting or scary numbers? How does it look in your organization or your hockey team?

If you would translate the above results into a hockey team with 5+1 players on ice, it would look like this:

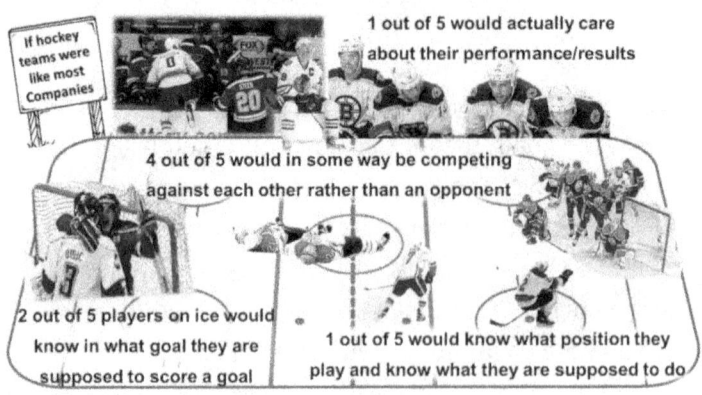

And for a full hockey team with 20 + 2 players:

8 out of 22 players would know in what goal to score in

4 out of 22 would care

4 out of 22 would know what position they are playing and what to do

18 out of 22 would somehow compete against each other rather than an opponent

You can only imagine the role of leading such a team! Nevertheless, these are real figures from large companies, and therefore a "reality".

Sometimes you can also reflect on how your hockey players would answer such a survey, maybe some areas would be ok, but others would not?

Working with clear goals, targets and a vision, connecting to each individuals contribution will align the company or a team, so let's continue the to look at how you can then steer the engagement in the right direction?

Goals / Direction
- Creating vision and setting goals

Focused direction of the energy

Most of us have had a magnifying glass, have you? I have. The original purpose of a magnifying glass is to visualize the details or make the details larger. Did you use the magnifying glass for something else?

I did...

I suppose you at least once tried to create a fire with your magnifying glass (when you were young)?

How can this be linked to (direction) your vision, goals and focused areas?

Your vision, goals and focused areas should do exactly the same work as the magnifying glass, capture the energy within the scope of the glass and focus the beams to one point, to create fire (why and what).

A message from the future

If we start with the vision, your target image 2-3 years away. First, you need to make it clear to yourself, why should you have a vision at all? What can it give you, your leadership and your team?

The vision gives you guidance in your leadership, coaching, daily decision-making, action and communication with the team, the players and with other coaches, parents, the club or the organization.

When you talk about a vision you and I can have different pictures in the head. I'll try to give you my picture. For me, to begin with, a vision can be in any format, only your own imagination can limit it. It can be anything from a few bullet points on a piece of paper to a short film "from the future".

So the format may not be so important, but it is more important how it is perceived, it should create energy alignment and direction in the long run, and to be honest how exciting are some sentences in bullet point form, even if they would do the job?

Vision - A versatile description of the future

A vision can be a colorful multidimensional description of what you as a leader see in the future, you can in your own head try to move a few years into the future and describe what you see, know, hear about the team, energy, motivation, goals, achievements , teamwork, team spirit, players, club, fans, results, behavior etc.

A good way to describe what has happened in the future is to actually try to describe as it would have happened, not in, "we should / should do / We need to".

The images you create are important (you will see in the lemon or basketball example later).

There is another dimension to add, our brains can't make a difference between created images and realistic real pictures. The difference comes from our own values and beliefs. If you can be open up to these new images, your brain will already accept the opportunity for future success.

I try to visualize the difference for you between some bullet points in meaning and when you really spend some time moving into the future and creating an attractive picture of the future desired position and situation.

Vision 2020

- We should win the league 2020

- We need to improve our team spirit

- We must increase the intensity in our practices

- We must make more goals on the opportunities we have

- We need to be faster in our game

- Etc.

Or...

May 8, 2022

I welcome you all to this press conference. I can imagine that you have many questions after our victory in the league. I start by giving you my view of the most important success factors, after which you will be able to ask some questions to the players.

To begin with, I think our victory would have not been possible without the fantastic team spirit we have in our team, we are there for everybody, all for one and one for all, to use an old expression! Everyone has had a clearly defined role, and all players have accepted this during this year or during these 3 years. We have not used the word "first line", we are a TEAM, where everyone had a clear task and have known what to do, and I mean it, you can ask the players.

During this year, we have increased the intensity of our training, which we also showed clearly in yesterday's last match in the series. We were the strongest team in the end, we were willing to go those extra meters, to do the back check, limit the space to pass on, and minimize the time for the opponent. If we look at how many goals we have made during the season, there are 89 goals, which also gives you the image of an aggressive, strong and fast team that can take advantage of the goal chances that we create!

The presentation may be that you actually rig a press conference with the players in the press role.

Do you see and feel the difference between these examples? Did you feel anything different when you read the second example? Do you want to be part of that team?

How was the first example, inspiring or just boring and tiring by all must and should?

The right target level and vision

The most important thing for me is to catch the players where they are and bring them on a "journey", which in many cases can be designed along the way. You as a coach can have, and should have, your dreams and visions of the future and burn for it, but pick up your players at the station where they are right now for the journey you are going to do together. But also remember to let go of the players who desire to do so, at the "right station".

If the rubber band is not strained, you have no one who follows you, if it is too tight, it goes off or hits you in the back...

Part two is to talk about which goals the player has long and short term? Why? Why is it important? Why does he / she want to get there?

SMART or "Outside the Box" Goals?

Have you heard of SMART goals (Specific, Measurable, Achievable, Realistic & Timely)? It is a way of thinking when setting goals, and it is also perhaps one of the most used words when talking about setting goals. But I will not dig deeper into SMART goals, at the moment, because I have problems with the word realistic, if you always think about, what is realistic, you will get stuck in old patterns and think in the old "historical patterns" and can achieve stable but somewhat slow progress. You do things that you have done before, just a little better.

Make the "unrealistic" goal realistic

Sometimes you need to create an imbalance in the structures with "unrealistic" goals, to get people to think outside the box and in new paths. In this case, it will not be enough to do things the way that we have always done, something more, new and drastically is needed. If the goal is too close to the last year's performance, you can continue in the same way and hope to achieve better results (via luck?)

When you introduce the new levels for goals or the new way of thinking when setting goals, you should also steer the dialogue towards, okay if you now believe that the goal is not realistic, what would we need to do (new things, more of, or less of) to make it more realistic? What would be the first step or area we need to improve? In which other areas do we need to improve to reach our goal?

We may have to take 100 small steps, and if we break it down and we identify 5 small things to do for each player, we will have one hundred small improvement steps of 20 players, to reach our new goal "outside the box."

Wanted position

To clarify the difference between the realistic inside the comfort zone and outside the box target (outside the comfort zone). You can divide the goal into two different categories to set goals, or how to look at the goal. The first is about looking back at your performance and setting the target a little higher than what history shows.

If you are considering goals for the league position you can look at your previous seasons e.g. 10th, 8th, 9th and therefore you think that a realistic goal should be 6 or 7, but you might choose to raise it a little bit, to reach at least position 5 and everyone would feel that it is realistic, because they know that no major improvements are needed, just some luck on the way?.

The other way to set goals is to take a step into the future and to think where you want to be in the future (what you want to achieve, vision) or where you need to be to achieve something. Let's say your team is in the second highest division. Perhaps you have described in your vision that you want to be in the top league, therefore you must automatically be top 2 or 3 in your division to be able to take the next step. This can create conflicts, if you have team members who are stuck in history, then they do not think this is a realistic goal, and it may not be for the moment, it is your desired position to take the next step. Remember the dialogue, do you want to be there? If so, what can we improve?

If you set goals by taking a step into the future and pointing to a desired position, you create an information gap that must be explained to the players, why do you think it is important, why is it important for the players? What's in for them? So the discussion with the players should rather be if they want to be there (in the top league), than if it is realistic. Once you have managed that discussion, you can start taking small steps back from the future to the present, if we want to be here, top 2 and advance a division. What changes do we need to make to achieve this? What should we start doing? What should we do more of? What should we stop doing? What new things should we do?

You have to cut the big step into small steps (We need to increase the amount of training. We need to think about what and how we eat. We need to improve our defense, we need higher intensity and speed.) When you have this discussion on many small improvements with your players, they become involved and committed to reaching the goal and suddenly it starts to be realistic at least in all heads. You can immediately, during the discussion, start writing down a list of improvements and focused areas coming from your players. Also, take the dialogue around each area, such as how do we increase the intensity, what can each one of us do?

You can think of José Mourinho's challenge when he set a goal that was to win the Champions League, when Inter had won it, by 1965, perhaps it was more realistic to look at other aspects than the historical performance, such as team members and Mourinho himself, but still they needed to improve a lot of areas, both physical and mental.

In short-term goals, you can use the same method to support your long-term goal and vision. What activities do we need to do closest, what activities can we start with immediately?

The final level is about focus areas that will support you to achieve your and your team's short-term goals (and ultimately, of course, the long-term goals and vision). What do we need to focus on as the first steps on the way to our desired position, areas that will help you towards the goals, e.g. block shots, shoot more, harder passes, quick turnovers etc.? This should of course be translated into concrete measures and act as a small mantra in different contexts, remember the focus area ... now during the training / match. Here is important to dare to prioritize, if you take too many areas, it will no longer be a focused area, if the focus should be everywhere. 1 is good, 3 is maximum.

As a summary, you can say that you can work on setting the direction at different levels, Vision - Long-term goals - Short-term goals - Focused areas - Measures / Action plan.

Measurable goals create energy and endurance over time

What is being measured gets done, clear goals will also increase the effort to reach the goals within the team. Your goals will serve as a guide for you when planning and prioritizing your activities for the team and, of course, the roadmap/journey becomes clearer when you know where you are heading.

Measurable goals

Try to talk about your goals, norms and rules as much as possible, as it will increase the performance and clarity of the goal and expectations on behavior. It will also be easier for you as a coach to evaluate the effort and give feedback if the goal is more specific. If you want to increase the puck control, you can set a goal of having at least ten successful passes from each player during a match, instead of saying, we need to increase the puck control (or to talk about what we should avoid, we should avoid losing the puck).

Use the goal for both training and match. Try to write down the goals and visualize it for the team. This ensures that you and your players have the same picture of what is measured and what is needed. If you only discuss and mention the goals, it will be possible that you do not have the same picture or you or your players forget about the goal and it can be interpreted in different directions, by each individual player as time goes by.

Common mistakes in goal setting

The goals are:

- Not followed up

- Not visualized

- Not specific

- Not understood

- Too many (too many goals will divide energy and focus)

If your goals and vision are strong enough, it will create energy and endurance over time.

"We should have a man on the moon before the end of the decade"

Goals / Direction
- Communication and Body language

Mourinho creates faith in the goals

José Mourinho is a good communicator and I think he can sometimes set the goals "outside the box" or non-realistic goals, but since he is such a good communicator, he makes his goals SMART from the very beginning through the way he communicates, he communicates a belief in the goals and explains why and creates the driving force among the players, the coach believes we can do it!

He is also very clear in his demands on the players, to reach the goals.

"Here, in every exercise, every match, every minute of your social life must center on the goal of being champion."
(In a letter from José Mourinho, sent to the players)

"I'm absolutely sure we'll be champions next season." / José Mourinho,

"Under normal circumstances, Porto will become champion, in abnormal conditions, Porto will also become champion" / José Mourinho, in the midst of the Portuguese premier league season.

Do we look at the same picture?

One of the most important things when we talk about vision, goals and focused areas is to communicate, as we already touched briefly.

How can you ensure that all players have the same goal or see the same image that you want to convey, or how do you know that the player has understood your message or seen the image you are trying to "paint" for them?

There will be many things that make the picture differ between your players, their experience, expectations, their own will, the language you use, including your body language and many other things. Therefore, it is important that you in some way get a receipt of their understanding and interpretation. If you also allow players to comment or perhaps add things to the vision, focus areas or goals, you will immediately get a stronger commitment from each of the players and a receipt of their understanding. Make the basic job with the target image, but involve the players in a dialogue about the direction and goals, and add good ideas and small rewordings according to the players' possible wishes.

The power of the dialogue

Involving your players in the vision and goal dialogue with questions, what do they think? Is this the right way? What is good? Does something need to be changed, why? Do not just accept that yes, ask questions, why do they think it is the right way, or why not, what did they think was exciting in the vision (and if not, why not?), Was there something that needs to be added or deleted, maybe the players have a good example that can be added to the story?

In the end, of course you are the one who decides on changes, but if you do not listen to your players, you must explain why you will not make changes, why continue with your "picture", but in that case you may also need to be prepared that you go alone against the vision or that you will have part of your team with you on that journey?

I can say that if the vision is well-founded, prepared and tested on a smaller group before the presentation, and it is attractive, you only get positive feedback and explanations why it is correct, maybe some good examples to strengthen it and therefore your players will feel that vision is also theirs.

In the dialogue you get, besides the players' involvement, perhaps valuable input which makes the vision picture even stronger, things that you had not thought of or did not feel were important, but for the team the added things were important.

Make some changes, they will probably not change the basic idea of your message and you will still have the same commitment from your team, in this case maybe even more, because you have added something and you as a leader showed them their opinion counts, you have shown respect for their knowledge, feelings, will and experience!

The same method can also be applied to hockey exercises, you explain, why do we have the exercise, what is the purpose and what is the problem that the players should solve and the framework (e.g. 2 vs 1), starting position and defined area on ice, but the how part the players stand for.

"I use a global method, I use direct methods to prepare our organization, but I also use guided discovery where I create the exercise, dictate the goal and the players come up with different solutions" / José Mourinho

Correct mental pictures

In the two examples with the vision, in bullet point form and the press conference, I showed you the difference between an attractive and maybe a less attractive vision, at least in my eyes.

How we formulate ourselves and what words we use to describe our goals and objectives (set the direction) will have a great impact on the players and the team. I will show you some more examples of why it is important to control focus and internal images through communication.

Our brains are amazing

Evonerye taht can raed this, rsaie yuor hnad ... not everyone can, but most can... and if you can't, you're still normal.

Olny tinhg taht is imopratnt is that the frist and lsat lteter are in the crorcet palce. Ohtreiwse it can be a mess and we can sitll raed it.

Take this with you in your leadership, our brains are amazing and will create images of what we say, even if we do not get the full picture or it is a mess with holes and gaps, our brains try to sort out and organize it and create an understandable picture of it, that may not always be 100% accurate.

No, no words in communication

Think of a moment when someone is talking to you and you felt that all the energy was gone at that moment or immediately afterwards. Do you have any such situation in your head, where you felt that all the energy was gone, maybe you got a mission that you had to do?

Think back to the words that the person used, can these have affected the energy loss? If there are energy losses in communication, you will probably not hear or feel that the direction is attractive either.

I think there are words that you can avoid in your communication, to reach out with your message in the best way. Do you have any examples of such negative words?

For me, the words, must, always, not and never, are some examples that can kill a message, or give the wrong kind of thinking. You can try to put these words in one sentence and think about the response from the recipient, by thinking about how you would react to the message yourself (you must always, then you can't... and never ...).

You can also use the "but word" to take the air out of a message / feedback. Great, but...

But can easily be changed to, "and" in many cases, such as, "good, AND you can ..." compared to, "good, BUT you can ..."

Let me give some examples of these negative destructive words, creating a wrong mental image (the wrong direction of your thoughts).

Don't think about...

Our goal is not to think of a yellow sour lemon, we should not think of yellow and you must avoid thinking of a yellow lemon! I think it's important to repeat it, don't think of a yellow lemon, we can't keep thinking about a yellow lemon all the time! We have to think of something other than a yellow lemon. Our goal is not to think of a yellow lemon!

What happened, what were you thinking about? You thought of a yellow lemon? Most of us do or would do with this type of communication, but that was not our goal of communication, right? Don't think of a LEMON!

Yet this is a very common way of communicating, we talk about what we should not do or not think about, with this way it is not natural to understand what we should actually do or think about instead, what is the natural opposite of a lemon? Or when we talk to young hockey players - not to do so (Don't do like that), how do they know what the correct way is?

Somehow our brains are built to sort out the important in a message (as in the example above with the letters), and so it is also with the word "not". The word does not usually fall into the sorting in the brain and we think of a yellow lemon, we create a clear picture of what we "should not" think about.

Do not shoot in the post, do not hit the post ... You know the result ... it will be the safest way to hit the post, we could just as well tell the brain, "hit the post".

"Focus should be on what to do and achieve, not on what to avoid"

Positive goal formulation

So like a little summary. It is important how the goals are formulated and communicated, try to formulate your goals in a positive way and avoid, sentences that contain "do not" and "must", these will create resistance, the word "not" sometimes disappears in our heads, DO NOT touch, freshly painted! What happens, you want to know if the fence / wall is actually painted? So just keep the positive parts of the goal formulation.

Feelings against facts

When talking about goals and direction, it is good to lean on facts so that our negative feelings and imagination do not take control of the situation.

Here is another example, when you are going to take a penalty shot you have to check your stress level, feelings and thoughts. You can also try to visualize facts, to control emotions and thoughts, did you know that to cover a football goal (soccer), you need 10 footballs over each other and 31 next to each other, which means you need 310 footballs to cover the whole goal. You have 310 places to shoot the ball into the goal or that there are about 75,000 places to place a tennis ball on the opponent's part of the plan. When we talk hockey, you need 1152 pucks to cover an ice hockey goal and in bandy you need 2040 bandy balls to cover a goal. It is not so difficult to make goals with these conditions?

"Think the thought, success starts with thinking the thought."

Basketball example

In basketball we all know that only one ball will fit into the basket. If you would ask someone who is not familiar with basketball, how much space will there be left outside the ball when it enters the basket ... by the way, what would you answer?

How many centimeters around the ball is there when it goes in the basket? If you place the ball in the middle, and measure from the edge of the ball to the ring, 2cm, 3cm or more?

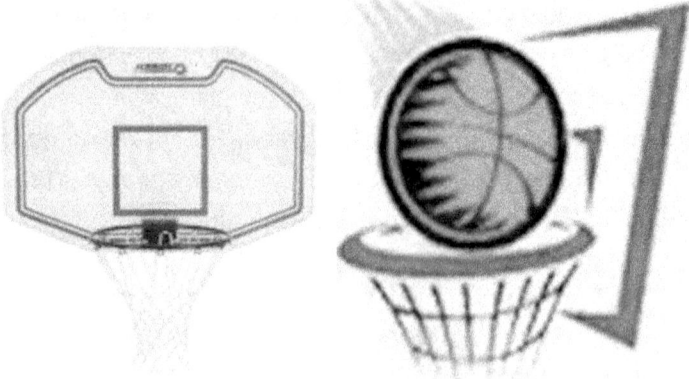

Of course, research has been done in this area. There were two teams of children who would compete against each other about which team that scores most free throws.

The first team had to stand on the floor and look up at the basketball basket and could then start throwing their basketballs. (Here you can make the parable at an unrealistic goal, which is only presented to the players).

The other team had a basketball basket on their level and could feel the size, measure the ball and even measure themselves into the basketball ring. They could see and feel with their own eyes how much space there was around the ball, they got facts and a feeling for what was required for the task, or to reach the goal, most balls in the basket. Then they started throwing the balls in the basket.

I think it is already quite obvious which of the teams might have worked better. Team one, with own created or given negative mental image of an inaccessible and difficult goal? Or team two with realistic fact-based positive image of reaching their goal?

I will also give you the right picture...

The answer is that you can almost get two basketballs (at least in women's size) in the basket at the same time.

It wasn't the picture you had in your head, right? Pretty big difference between these two pictures? You can imagine how easy it will be for you the next time you play basketball, or imagine the effect on your players when they have the right image and not be guided by negative thoughts and feelings when starting a new exercise, training or working against one common goal.

Everything is possible, use facts to remove negative emotions and thoughts and work on changing negative to positive, "... but," to "and", "think if I ..."/"what if I ..." to "why not"?

Positive or negative effect of your message?

Choose your words wisely. You can say things in a negative way or in a creative positive way. Why tell the players how they should not do things or what to avoid, when you can choose to talk about how and what they should do and what opportunities they have. Words that you say as leaders affect your players, their mental images and the culture within the team (direction of their behavior).

If you throw something in the water, you can see the rings it will create on the water surface, rings that spread and become larger. Therefore, carefully select the words and messages that you "throw" into your team. Every action, word, behavior, attitude, activity counts within the team, these things will spread throughout the team in one way or another, you can decide which rings are spreading and which strengthen the behavior in the direction you want and how your team will work together.

Mental homework

This can also be a lesson to your players, trying to control or change their own negative thoughts that they face in other situations outside of hockey towards positive thoughts. Discuss with the players about the task and let them also discuss with each other how to think to break negative thought paths.

They need to train these skills as much as technical skills with a puck. If you want to be a master, you have to think like one.

Take full responsibility for your own thoughts, there is no room for negative thoughts in a successful team. Your thinking drives your behavior and actions and these will create your performance and direction for your energy.

How are you as a leader, are you emotionally controlled or fact based, do you have a negative or positive tone in your communication? What words do you use in your communication?

Synchronized video and audio

Communication and your body language are important when talking or having a dialogue with your players, regardless of subject or problem and saying the same thing as your body language shows or vice versa.

Verbal and body language

Good communicators are effective both verbally and through body language. Their body language strengthens the message and matches the verbal message, you can watch Mourinho. Just look at the body language and you will almost hear what he says? Have you thought of your own body language when communicating, how is it when you are happy or excited?

A matching and "exciting" body language reinforces your message, of course it must not go to exaggeration, because then you lose the message...

This can be something to take with you (matching body language) when communicating with your players, e.g. When you talk about the goal of the team or when you introduce a new exercise, show a little over movements and feelings. Many of them will link your body language and face expressions to a positive feeling unconsciously and therefore also be better listeners.

Try to present something with your arms crossed on your chest and end with, okay, let's have fun and reach our goals, would you be trustworthy?

Make sure your video and audio are synchronized!

"The coach's face is a mirror of the team's health" Arséne Wenger

Goals / Direction
- Visualization

Another important thing about goals is visualization. Visualize the goals in a good way to help your players focus their energy and keep them motivated. Visualization makes the road visible, towards the goal.

Visualize your goals

You do not always need to have exact figures when you want to view or review the overall performance towards the goals and targets. For example, you can use faces or hockey players in different colors to visualize goals and performance at the moment.

Green smiling hockey face, you are on target. Yellow neutral face, you are in the right direction, but may need to take some action. Red sad face, improvement measures are needed. Immediately everyone can have the same picture about the current state and about the need for any improvements on the future path towards the goal.

Take a photo when you make a goal

Green, yellow and red faces are one way to visualize, another may be that you ask someone to take pictures of the audience or your team when you play, take a picture when you score a goal during the match, and it will be the team's, "on the right path towards the target image". A good goal chance can visualize "almost on target" and a neutral game situation, will symbolize that you have some "improvements to make".

You can, and perhaps should, use this method for both short and long term goals. If you have a neutral picture of the long-term goal, you can at least have some positive images for the latest win or performance in the last game or the latest hockey training.

The small steps are important to visualize, keep the team spirit up and have faith and motivation to achieve the long-term goals and vision.

Use your imagination and not be limited by this example. What examples are in your head, how can you make the visualization, triggering your players?

"I am very happy that the club is making a record of the sale of new match jerseys. I do not sell jerseys, but there is a relationship between sweater sales and the team's performance. If we perform well, they sell more jerseys."

/Mourinho

Goals / Direction
- Norms, values and rules

Norms create team culture

Still on the theme, what sets the direction for behavior within the team? When you look at this area you will naturally enter the area with rules, values and norms within the team.

If you search for the word, the norm in Wikipedia, you will find the following explanation. "Social norms are behaviors within a society or group or the" hidden" rules that a group uses for appropriate and inappropriate values, beliefs, attitudes and behaviors."

The norms will affect both the focus within the team and the collaboration within the team.

Norms can be divided into different categories, here are some examples.

- Descriptive norms - govern the behavior of the team.

- Value norms - helps the team prioritize among the desired behavior.

- Discrete norms - not visible when followed, but if someone violates a norm, it becomes visible, someone goes in the wrong direction.

To develop, visualize and strengthen the desired norms and behavioral direction within the team, you can use various team building activities, discussions and feedback as some of your tools.

Norms are usually linked to behavior before, after and during practices, matches, regular season and in social situations. One of the common norms in all teams will be the expectation of how hard you are expected to work during an practice or a match. Is it ok to go out on the ice "on one skate" (not full speed)? Or just "join" the defensive game?

These are topics that sometimes require coaching and support from you as the leader to address it in a correct way and with right tone level within the team and between team members.

Norms within a group of monkeys

Here is an experimental example of monkeys and how they create and handle norms within the group.

- There were a group of monkeys who lived in a large cage, every day the monkeys were given bananas, which were hung high up in the tree that was located in their enclosure. Directly when the bananas had been hung up in the tree, one of the monkeys set off to pick them up, a natural behavior. (Energy - why do something? The monkeys need food / bananas to survive, direction - what is the purpose? Take down the bananas to be saturated, me and the group). This was repeated several times, but then one day, when one of the monkeys is about to bring down the bananas from the tree, all other monkeys are washed with water, they become very wet and if there is something that monkeys do not like, it is water.

After a while, a new monkey heads up to the tree to bring down the bananas from the tree, with the same result, wet monkeys.

Having repeated this several times, the monkeys understand the message, they continue with theirs, without trying to bring down the bananas from the tree.

After a while they start replacing the old monkeys / group members with new monkeys. The new monkey directly discovers the bananas and head towards the tree, to bring them down (natural behavior, monkeys love bananas), but even before the new monkey has reached the tree, he is brutally stopped by the group. Don't touch the bananas! They know the consequences, go after the bananas, equals with wet monkeys. The new monkey adjusts to the team.

In the end, all the original team members have been replaced, but the monkeys still do not touch the bananas. They still stick to the old norm, do not touch the bananas in the tree, without knowing why, it is as it is, and has always been. Do you recognize this from real situations?

"This is how we do things here, it has always been so, so don't come with any changes"

Norms tend to live long

We are governed many times by rules, norms and guidelines because we think they are meaningful, but the logic can sometimes be old-fashioned and not relevant anymore, but the norms affect the social direction and create a culture within the team or the club, positive or negative that will control the behavior for a long time.

How does it look in your team or your club? Is it clear why you do or do not do things or why people act in a certain way? What norms exist in the background? What kind of positive norms can you introduce? Is it ok to try new things and fail even in important situations in the end of an important game?

Outspoken rules

If the norms are more invisible, the rules are more obvious and visible. Rules can, as the norms be divided into certain categories, here are some examples.

- How- or framework rules - framing in what is okay and what is not, generally (controlling behavior).

- Prioritizing rules - when you need to choose or make your own decisions, you know the team priorities (control priorities)

- Time rules - elimination of collaborative losses (controlling behavior)

Mourinho's rules in Real Madrid

When José Mourinho started his journey with Real Madrid, you could read about some of his rules in the newspapers.

- Don't come late, I'm not waiting for anyone.

- The training starts at 9:30. Those who come late are locked out from the rest of the team and may train individually.

- The bus always leaves on time. If a player is late, he is left at home, even if it is a minute's delay.

- Injured players should come to the training one hour before the training begins. After examination, the doctor should then report to Mourinho about the situation.

- The training is always 90 minutes long.

- Mobile phones can be used on the bus. But the signal must be silent, so the rest of the squad will not be disturbed by incoming calls.

"I'm not waiting for anyone, even if it means we will play the game with a man less" / José Mourinho

Feedback to Benzema about following the rules of the team

Spanish Marca wrote that Mourinho repeatedly held talks with Benzema about discipline and the rules.

"If it was only for you, I would have the training in the middle of the day, because you come here at ten, half asleep, and at eleven you have already fallen asleep again" / Mourinho

Maybe little bit off topic, but did you know that a space shuttle uses more energy the first three minutes after a start than during the entire trip?

Make sure you have the right amount of energy and the right direction when you start, because you will struggle against gravity in the form of old behaviors, norms, thinking and habits, unless you have the ability to set the direction from the beginning.

Stress level affects focus and attention

The focus during the match or training can also take different forms. Too high or low level of stress / excitement will affect many areas, one of which is the focus. When we talk about focusing, you can talk about optimal, wide or narrow focus.

1. Optimal attention, with moderate or optimal arousal / stress level with which the player is comfortable. The players can then see both opportunities and possible obstacles.

2. Too wide attention fields, as a result of low excitement. Focusing on something other than the situation, the energy spreads on many things.

3. Too narrow attention field, due to very high arousal. Limited to one option and only see the obstacles, can not have any other solutions.

Creativity within the framework

Give your team members goals, not instructions on how to reach them, coach and guide towards the goal. Ask for their solutions and skills to reach the goal. Give the players room to act and thus also space for creativity, within the framework that you have created.

You do not need to have all the answers, guide and coach your players to answers within themselves (e.g. players: how should we do this? Coach: do you have a good proposal how to do it? Or how would you like to solve it? Has someone else a solution?) After starting the fire / energy and creating a purpose for it (why and what), avoid putting your fingers in the fire (how), creating the framework of the fire and trusting your players and guiding through a coaching attitude.

"I use a global method, I use direct methods to prepare our organization, but I also use guided discovery where I create the exercise, dictate the goal and the players come up with different solutions" / José Mourinho

Decide on a training idea

Many hockey coaches do not have their own training idea or training philosophy (direction / vision for me as coach, what do I stand and aim for) and only every third dare to stick to it in the long run.

Have you thought about you leadership or hockey cornerstones? What do you stand for? How do you want to work? What are your leadership values and rules?

This is a good reflection exercise, think about the leadership model in this book and apply it on your own way of acting and doing things.

Dare to stand for your basic training principles and your direction in your leadership, it will be a lot easier if you have clarified and also maybe written this down for yourself.

"Individually skilled skaters and creative players with great team spirit

I use the ice time with quality. I create opportunity for development and creativity. Good skaters have time to be creative and find solutions to problems during the matches. "Creative Mistakes" can be repaired with good skating..."

Teamwork

Leadership responsibility		Teamwork			Team Responsibility
Energy / Engagement	Direction / Goals	Capacity	+ Team Spirit	- Collaboration losesses	Results (Hard and soft)
Feedback and learning					

Teamwork (capacity + team spirit) – Collaboration losses

Leadership responsibility		Teamwork		Team Responsibility	
Energy / Engagement	Direction / Goals	Capacity	+ Team Spirit	- Collaboration losesses	Results (Hard and soft)
Feedback and learning					

Category: Teamwork

Teamwork = (Capacity + team spirit) – Co-operational losses

The third block is about teamwork, how you and your players work together.

The three parts in the middle are about teamwork within the team during training, match and outside, the parts come from Steiner's model with small changes, it describes the group's cooperation and the conditions for achieving results. The Steiner model is based on what we can strengthen within our team, capacity and team spirit and try to minimize the third, collaborative losses.

Capacity can be defined e.g. such as training and utilization of knowledge, skills, physical, mental skills, equipment, facilities, training times and training opportunities etc.

Team spirit can sometimes be difficult to define, it is something that is in the group and that makes the team stronger. Togetherness, clear roles, security, appreciation, positive climate, community, common vision and goals can be

115

some keywords when we talk about team spirit, 1 + 1 becomes more than two.

Collaboration losses can involve, for example, unclear roles, incorrect positions on the plan, bad passes, unsynchronized activities, in short, all "errors" that complicate and impair the team. Collaboration losses consist mainly of two categories, loss of co-operation and motivational losses.

Motivation losses tend to occur when the team size increases, or when the leader does not see all the players, then you suddenly do not get 100% from each team member, this phenomenon is called social loafing, I am not important and I do not need to do my best, my performance will still not be visible.

"We have top-class players and, sorry if I sound arrogant, we have a top-class trainer"

/ José Mourinho

"I think we all believe we're going back for Game 7," the Blues coach said. "Why wouldn't we? We're a confident group, we've played good hockey for a long time, and we're going to continue to play good hockey here today."

/Craig Berube

Teamwork
Capacity

Leadership responsibility				Team Responsibility	
		Teamwork			
Energy / Engagement	Direction / Goals	Capacity	+ Team Spirit	- Collaboration losesses	Results (Hard and soft)
Feedback and learning					

Teamwork - Play hockey together

Is it possible to predict the possibility of success for a team? I say it is. This teamwork block and the parts in it are about predicting a performance and the opportunity to deliver results. The teamwork block consists of three parts, (capacity + team spirit) - collaboration losses = the team's performance.

The first part, capacity is one of the parts you should try to strengthen with your hockey training and practices, but there are other aspects to consider as well.

In capacity you can enter:

- Training facilities

- The number of hockey training

- Exercise length

- How to use practice time

- The quality of the training and exercises

- Training equipment

- Skills

- Experience

- Support around the team, assistant coach, goalkeeper coach, material/equipment manager, physio coach, doctor etc.

A little thought about the leadership roles. You always have a head coach in hockey, assistant coaches, coaches for the defense, goalkeeper coaches and other support functions around the hockey team, but who is the "goal scoring coach"? A little important thought?

The easiest part to copy between teams

The easiest part to improve or at least get the right conditions from the start in the big clubs is probably the capacity block and now I'm talking about the teams in the highest leagues. You have good players and the opportunity to acquire new ones, there are good training opportunities, you have everything in place around the team, and this is the part that is also easiest to "copy" between the teams, the second part connecting to the culture or team spirit will be much harder to just "copy" from someone else, it needs to created, just like the work with energy and direction.

Of course, some clubs have better financial conditions to get this in place, but unlimited money will not bring you natural success, there are many failures with clubs that get a lot of money and unlimited resources to buy players, but the victories will still not come. Then you have problems with other parts of the leadership model, such as team spirit, collaboration losses, motivation or common goals...

Looking at an example from football, Roberto Mancini (2010) in Manchester City, suddenly had almost unlimited money to spend on players and at the beginning of the season he had bought five left-defensemen and he had also ten "defensive" midfielders. That means some other players have to leave, or take on new roles (there is not room for 10 defensive midfielders), worse when too many big stars get too little game time or attention.

The question is, did Mancini buy capacity or collaboration losses?

Other aspects to consider in this section are the roles of your players. When we talk about roles, a role is defined by expectations from the coach, teammates and how you feel yourself that you want to live up to those requirements (more on this later).

"Karim Benzema must understand that he does not play for himself, he must be a team player and work very hard, especially on training." / José Mourinho

Some other quotes, related to capacity:

"It's like having a blanket that is too small for the bed. You pull up the blanket to keep your chest warm and your feet protrude. I can't buy a larger blanket because the supermarket is closed. But I'm happy because the blanket is cashmere. It's no ordinary blanket. " / José Mourinho

"We are at the top of the moment but not because of the club's financial power. We are involved in the battle for many trophies because of my hard work." / José Mourinho

Resources and capacity round the team and for the team is one thing, but the big thing is to build the players individual hockey capacity through quality practices and matches.

Practice vs. Match

Many hockey players and parents often think about whether matches or practices help a player to develop the most (build capacity)? Take a look at the facts below and you will have the answer to what is best in terms of player development.

One of the biggest problems with the development of hockey players is how many practices they have compared to the number of matches they play. An ideal and realistic relationship is 2 training sessions for each match played in ages 7-13. Keep in mind that your players can practice hockey almost anywhere. You do not have to wait for a scheduled ice practice to practice hockey skills and all training does not have to be done on ice. Encourage your players to train at home and with friends.

Guidelines for a 60-minute Ice Training:

If you get into an effective hockey training with good intensity as well, it gives a hockey player more skills development than 11 hockey games. If so, you should:

Strive for each player to have a puck on the stick for 8 - 12 minutes during each hockey training.

Strive to have each hockey player to have at least 30 shots on goal during each hockey training. Young hockey players will miss the goal in over 30% of the shots during a hockey exercise, work on the focus.

Aim to have 4-5 different hockey drills on each hockey training. It doesn't necessarily get better with more drills, focus on the performance and the quality of what you do on your hockey training. That develops your players.

Do not use the ice time for long feedback sessions. Aim that a maximum of 5 minutes per practice is for review. It can be difficult, but try to have it as a target.

If you have 10 hockey players on the ice, try to keep 4-5 hockey players activated all the time during the hockey exercise.

If you have 15 hockey players on the ice, strive to keep 9 - 10 players hockey players activated all the time during the hockey exercise.

If you have 20 hockey players on the ice, strive to keep 14-15 players hockey players activated all the time during the hockey exercise. (think of the different roles you can add to a drill, more about this in the book Multidimensional Hockey Training).

A hockey match in numbers:

The following statistics symbolize a hockey match that takes 60 minutes to complete (2x15 min = 50 min, 2x20 min = 60-70 min)

• Hockey players will have the puck on the blade in average of 8 seconds per player and match.

• Hockey players take an average of 1-2 shots per match.

• 99% of the feedback from the coaches is to players when they have the puck. Ironically, hockey players only have the puck on their stick in 0.2% of the hockey game.

Then you can also easily see the effect of a shot plate at home, when it comes to the above figures, 30 shots on a 60 minute workout, the same amount of shots are carried out, with ease with no more than 10 minutes on the shooting plate at home. Thoughtful and effective for capacity building!

Shot and skills training at home provides tremendous effect, if possible

So if you look at the statistics, you realize the importance of training in the right relationship with matches and that the practices are effective.

Studies also show that the better the children are at something, the more they will enjoy it, and the longer they will play. Many children end up with hockey because they come to the level where they cannot compete because lack of skills - therefore it is no longer fun. That situation does not seem to occur with the console games?

Of course, the matches are extremely important from several aspects, but from a developmental point of view, training gives more.

At age 5 - 6 or 5 - 7, the training relationship should be even higher (6: 1) and realistically, formal matches are not always necessary.

My goal for the training

"Individually skilled skaters and creative players with team spirit" Use the ice age with quality. Create opportunity for development and creativity. Good skaters have time to be creative and find solutions to problems during the matches. "Creative Mistakes" can be repaired with good ice skating...

Exercise length 60-80 minutes, focusing on skating.

15-20 minutes skating skills (with and without puck)

20-25 minutes station training (other skills).

5-10 minutes of skate (relay, play etc.).

10-15 minutes small team play in three zones.

In order to be able to focus on skating techniques on the ice practice, you can move some exercise moments to outside the ice, such as stick handling. Off-ice exercises with a wooden ball can be performed in groups or individually before and / or after the ice training.

The development process is long-term

It is also important to see the training and development process (capacity building) as long-term, the elite level will very few reach, but many can be on the journey for a long time.

To keep the flame alive, it is often enough with small means, such as seeing each individual and positive feedback can create miracles.

The role of parents in sport and development

The parents play a major role in children's and young people's sports. All parents want their children to succeed and be good at what they are doing. As a leader, it is important to keep track of the children's own will, but also the parents' will and purposes, and sometimes guide the will in the right direction.

It is important to take the child forward in the development where he or she is currently, not stand by the "own goal" (professionals) and push on. Supporting, driving to practice and supporting financially are the most important factors for the parents.

It is important that everyone sees and lets the children train on their own terms and allows other sports in addition to the "own" favorite sport. Versatile training benefits your child and us leaders in a special sport.

What role does the team and the coaches have?

Being a coach for children and young people differs significantly at one point towards being a coach for an adult team, the educating part (part of capacity building, outside hockey).

Sport has always had a raising role and will have in the future, but children and young people need other adults, not least their own parents, but also guidelines and frameworks for "life" from school and from other sports.

 The role of sports clubs in society is, according to me, significant. There, friendship is created for life, an improved basic physics, hopefully good basic values, norms, understanding of how to work and act in group and team work, as well as new elite athletes, but also hopefully new coaches, leaders and referees are raised.

Being a Coach is a Hobby - Why?

Why is the coaching and leadership role for young people in sports regarded many times as a hobby activity, it is probably no, or at least not many, who see it as a "real" work, even though it often corresponds to at least half-time work (just look at the fictitious job advertisement at the beginning of the book). What is really the difference between being a coach to working at a school or preschool? Except the majority of hockey coaches are not paid (at least not in Sweden and Finland)

The same ingredients and work are required. Plan and prepare the training or lesson, bring out stuff, create groups, help dress, tie skates, carry out training, give feedback, show how it works, create a creative environment, help undress, pick up, leave back the children to the parents, clean, dot off the presence, prepare the matches... Being a leader for adults is demanding, but training children and young people has more dimensions.

Being a leader and trainer for children is a profession that requires education, unfortunately it is probably not the case in many times. Nothing bad about the parents, but unfortunately there are too many who take on the coaching role, but without a real coaching training, sometimes with some or great experience from playing themselves, but it is not equal to being able to teach in the right way. (Build on the capacity part)

Can you get help from outside to strengthen the capacity part?

What should the club or team do itself and what can you buy or rent in when it comes to training and leadership to build the capacity? An area where the hiring of expertise skills has always been strong is within the goalie training, but why not take in expert help for the skate training, goal scoring, the small team game etc. The optimal would of course be to hire "half-professional" coaches for the smallest, which is where the basics are laid for "own products" / own players, which most clubs talk about. This is a part that has a clear growth right now.

Look at the leadership model or the details in each block to address the correct area to get support in.

Teamwork – Capacity
- Off season

Hockey Then and Now connected to capacity

The pace of the hockey and the speed of performance is the difference in today's hockey compared to earlier. Work with frequency and speed of execution, the time to do things decreases all the time.

Capacity - The activity level among children and young people dropping

The activity level of children and young people has fallen terribly scary, which naturally affects capacity. A recent study in Finland shows that even active children in sports teams just pass the bar for recommended activity.

 The goal for a 12-year-old and older is to train 18 hours a week (be physically activated, in other words not just organized training).

The surveying group (active athletic children) only average 13.4 hours a week, this means that a 16-year-old athlete will miss about 2,000 hours against the goal, important to remember when we start talking about the 10,000 hours later. The lack of training and good physics also begins to appear to the team coaches.

The lack of basic physics for children and young people

The poor or lack of basic physics of the children and young people gives completely different types of challenges to the coaches in the team. The trainer will find it difficult to, for example, start teaching skating technique, if it is difficult to get down in a squat position.

Or to practice more advanced steps of skills, if both physics and coordination are several years after the actual age. Looking for underlying causes for the inactivity is not particularly difficult?

... or is it that children today have completely different types of talent and skills with them and that the coaches have not understood it yet? (More about this topic in the book "Multidimensional Hockey Drills and Training")

"NHL Highlights on the mobile" - another type of capacity is built up

134

To train children and young people

Exceptional performances are becoming evident further down in the ages, even if some of the children devote more time to the mobile and gaming consoles, then there are also those who carry out technical tasks that many adult players could not imagine themselves performing five years ago or exhibit a technical level, which they never themselves were nearby in the same age, even though they are world stars

today. A strange equation, less physical activity for the majority, but higher speed, more advanced skills and quicker decision making. Maybe the lack of physics is covered up by a quick and "well trained" brain "thanks to" console games and mobiles?

With the development, people around the world have begun to focus more on youth training and leadership, as this creates the strongest foundation for elite sports later in life. However, being alone is not enough when it comes to youth training. The trainer's own interest and expertise should arouse the interest and the inner drive of those he or she is training, actually without creating pressure or forced situations, what an exciting challenge?

How important is off season training for a hockey player?

Hockey players are created on the ice, but the physical foundation on the off-ice training and especially the physical skills creates an athlete. When ice and off-ice training goes hand in hand, you can create an elite player in the complex sports hockey, with good physical capacity.

Physics cannot be equated with better hockey players, but versatile physics and good physical skills give everyone the opportunity to become a better hockey player. The versatile training and control of your own body is most important. Training hard sometimes, "to the puke limit" is like training in itself and as training for the future, in order to reach the elite, hard work is required, but not all the time.

In the younger years, coordination, balance, speed (frequency) and resilience are the keys.

Strength training can also be carried out with your own body, or by increasing the load, for example, by using the nature, i.e. use a slope for running and for jumping.

The complex sport of hockey - how do you put it into off season training?

I mentioned earlier that hockey is a complex sport, you can easily understand that it requires a lot and versatile training to build up the capacity block.

In hockey you not only perform a repetitive "locked movement", but hockey is about a combination of interlinked movements and skills. We can take an example, just before a scoring situation: Fast skating forward (reaction speed, skating speed), pass reception (eye-hand coordination), pass with lateral movement (eye-hand-body coordination, balance and weight transfer), shot in motion (speed, explosive force, balance and weight transfer).

Interlinked physical skills

Hockey is about interconnected movement patterns where the various physical skills are linked together or used simultaneously. That is why this way of thinking also needs to be included in the planning and design of off-ice practices and training.

An example, standing on one foot will be managed by most

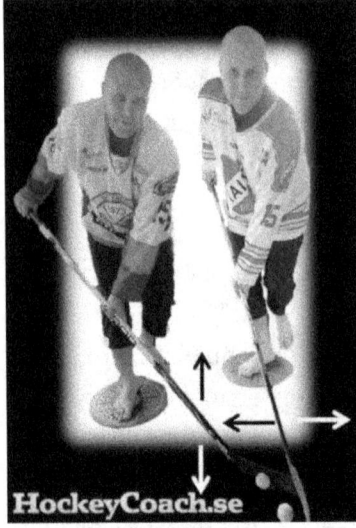

people pretty easily, so that exercise does not give much in itself to most, but if you do e.g. the same exercise standing on toes, on one leg, it becomes more difficult and at the same time you "plug in" the calf muscle into the training, in addition to a more advanced balance exercise, if you also close your eyes, you have taken it one step further, other options for connecting more skills are jumping forward/backwards, of course with the eyes open or jump on one leg, sideways, balance on a balance board etc.

Versatile off-ice training - some things to think about

In an effective off-ice training for hockey players, the body is used in every possible way, with different force and intensity, rhythm (calm - explosive) and movements in all directions (forward, backward and lateral).

Instead of "just" doing the plank (front hold, hover, or abdominal bridge), you can run it in pairs in a combat moment and thereby activate more skills.

A well-trained hockey player

All players are not well-trained, it's true, but it's also true that all good hockey players are. A good and versatile physical capability gives you or your hockey players the keys to succeed and everything starts from the individual player. It is their own drive that needs to be in order to succeed.

If you look at the areas that you need to develop off-ice, you can divide this into five physical basic parts, coordination, speed, mobility, strength and endurance. A hockey player do not need not be the best in any of this in comparison to other sports, however, you need to be really good at all five, to be a well-trained hockey player.

As a hockey coach, you need to understand and have skills in off season training in addition to everything that is to happen on the ice. If you do not know how the body reacts to different loads, you need to be lucky to succeed, and hoping for luck in training is rarely a good combination. You need that skill yourself, but your players need it more. Support them in getting their own drive for the physical exercise.

Interval training in Hockey

Previously, hockey players were running 5-10 km or more during an off season practice, now the interval thinking from on ice practices is applied in off season training and many do not run no more than 600 meters at a time. 4 x 200 meters gives more than one hour on exercise bike.

Training models to build up physical capacity

You can simplified say that there are two general approaches to training methods. The first is about making a large number of repetitions, sets and exercises per muscle group. 50-70%, 10-15 repetitions X 5-10 sets and> 4 exercises per muscle group

The second approach is more similar to that used for maximum strength training. 70-80%, 6-10 repetitions X 3-5 sets and <4 exercises per muscle group.

Strength Training

	Load %	Number of reps.	Number of sets	Rest (min)
Maximum strength	85-100	1-3	2-5	3-5
Muscle growth	70-80	8-12	3-6	2-4
Explosive strength	70-85	4-6	3-6	2-4
Speed strength	40-70	6-10	3-6	2-4
Endurance strength	40-60	15-50	2-4	30 sec – 2 min
Learning	Light	8-12	2-4	2

Speed Training

	Load %	Work (sec)	Rest (min)	Number of reps.	Number of sets
Frequency	Max	5-20	1-2	4-6	1-3
Accelaration	Max	3-20	30 sec – 3 min	5-6	1-3
Maximum	Max	5-8	1-8	5-6	1-3

Endurance Training (Aerob / Anaerob)

	Load %	Work (sec)	Rest (sec)	Number of reps.	Number of sets
Short-Short intervall	85-100	10-20	10-15	20-60	1-5
Short intervall	85-100	30-90	15-30	10-25	1-3
Long intervall	85-100	2-10 (min)	1-5 (min)	2-10	1-2
Speed endurance (anaerob)	Max	10-20	3-6 (min)	2-5	1-3
Max. speed endurance (anaerob)	Max	20-90	2-15(min)	2-10	1-2

A good format in off season training is to work with stations or circular training that activate different types of muscles.

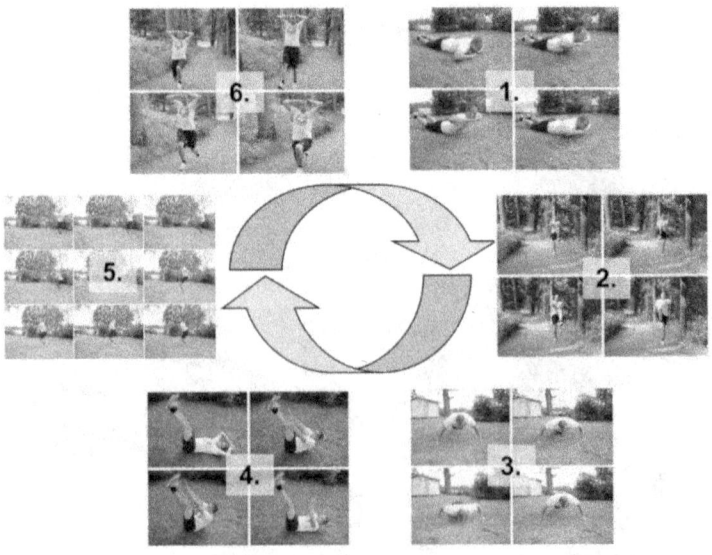

Above examples of possible layouts for circular training: 1. Upper body - back 2. Legs / jumps 3. Upper body - arms 4. Upper body - stomach 5. Jump / coordination / Entire body 6. Legs

One-sided off season training will increase the risk of injury, if you do not activate all the small support muscles and you will not be as good hockey player as you had become with more versatile training.

Jump hurdles during off ice training

We take a classic off-ice example:

6 series of jumps over 10 hurdles, with recovery on the way back.

Why do we do this?

What do we want to achieve / strengthen?

How? If you go with this exercise with hurdles, you need to consider, if the distance between the hurdles is "correct" and is the height correct on the hurdles?

To avoid narrow minded exercises, you need to think about how hockey really is, as I have been into before. On the ice, things happen all the time which must be taken into account and reacted on, skills must be linked and executed with precision. Versatile challenge for the body and combinations of skills in the exercises are the key, balance together with strength / coordination, combat moments / strength, jump / balance etc.

Development of jumping hurdle exercise

If we return to the "jump-hurdle" example, instead of doing, 6 series with jumps over 10 hurdles, an alternative could be to insert steps between, zick-zack running - jump - running with spin around - jump - backwards running - jump - somersault - jump.

Another example could be to start in pairs, shoulder towards shoulder (push) - lateral movement (pull and brake) - jump (each one hurdle) - lateral movement one pulls the other brakes - lateral movement - jump.

Does hockey suffer from unilateral training?

Suffers according to me. Early specialization and tight off ice exercises, often with power straight ahead. Many do not think about why and what you train for, the picture is just, that now we run tough and like this we have done before or when I was a player we did so, of course I do not speak for the whole hockey community with that claim, but this is yet widespread. Consider the previous example with hurdles and how you can apply the same kind of thinking to other exercises.

Other sports, other muscle groups and game understanding

The important thing that I think most sports are losing is that game understanding, other muscle groups and coordination are also available from other sports! Other sports contribute to hockey's capacity blocks in this model.

 In the US and Canada they have a stricter seasonality in sports, compared e.g with Nordic countries, which opens up for other sports in the summer, such as Lacrosse, American football, football (soccer) and athletics, the team is not collected for 10-11 months a year and structured in the same way. The season often starts with a try-out, which in itself creates a mentality to be better than the opponent, but also to be better than the team mate and it obviously characterizes the attitude to all training. Positive or negative?

The training should still be technically, tactically, and quantity wise right for the age level. Lots of technical and tactical moments can be "hidden" in playful exercises, it is possible to have fun while exercising properly and hard, no matter how long the season is.

Strive for many teams to practice off ice in the same location

If you can get several teams to train in the same location during e.g. the pre-season (off season), the youngest players can see how the older players put down great force and are serious in their training.

The adult and junior players are already idols in some way for the younger players and when training simultaneously or in succession, good habits can easily be transferred from the elderly to the younger ones. They see that they will need hard work now and in the future.

Off season training then and now

Previously, the exercise was summed up after a training week with the number of kilos of "scrap" that the players had lifted or the number of kilometers that had been covered.

Nowadays, fitness training goes more and more on exercises and strength training with your own body as a load. The own body is used together with combination movements and the waist support muscles are trained and taken care of more carefully than the hockey stick taping prior to an ice practice.

Individually strong, moving and explosive players are equal to a better team.

Teamwork – Capacity - Skating

Skating foundation for everything

Now in the capacity part the focus has in the beginning been, on off-ice. Let's move to on-ice and start with skating and skating skills, this is really the basis of all other hockey activities, stickhandling, fakes, passing the puck, pass reception, shots and all other game situations.

Skating is a prerequisite for being able to perform these tasks without having to think and focus, for example, on the balance or on moving forward, it goes and should go automatically. Without good skating all other areas in hockey will suffer.

Dave Smith, the NHL referees "boss", showed an interesting example during a coach training, you ask the players to start running on the spot, doing stickhandling and then you as a coach start asking questions to the players, this will visualize how automated the moves are, quick responses, automatized.

If the responses are slow, even if you are only running and not on the ice, the combined movements (running on the spot doing stickhandling) are requiring too much from the brain, decision-making will be even slower during a match. More training, in order to automatize the moves!

Skating

Skating can be divided into a number of base areas, which are balance, stride, physics, feeling and skating position.

Skating varies and will vary between different individuals, but everyone needs to be able to move smoothly on the ice, it is from skating, everything starts from. No skating, no success.

The balance in skating

It is enough to look at the skate or edge contact surface with the ice, to realize that balance is one of the cornerstones of good skating.

A narrow edge that is a number of millimeters wide and has a total contact area with the ice of 4-6 cm, this is the base of the "reversed pyramid".

Through this contact surface, the player should go full speed forward, backward, turn, stop, make direction changes, resist body contact and pushes, while the player has an eye on the puck, fellow players, opponents and the game in general.

Put time on balance and coordination exercises, outside, but also on the ice.

Good exercises include inner edge, outer edge, skating on one leg with turns and various combinations of these. Picture to left, jumping from backwards one foot inner edge to forward skating.

Instead of just doing regular squat, you can combine it with a jump from the squat position.

The difficulty of the inner edge practice is increased by having the glove, elbow or one knee on the ice.

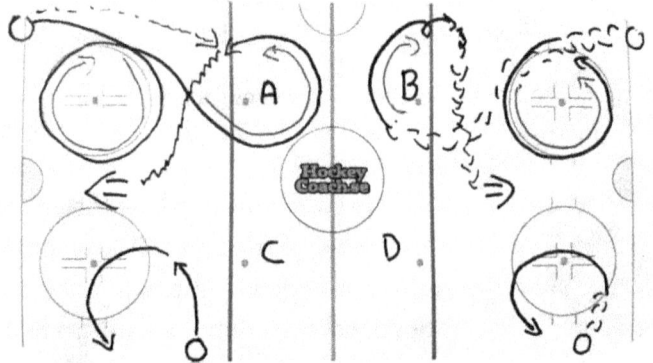

Hockey drill A: Round the circle (inside edge, one foot), with knee / glove / elbow in the ice, repeat outside blue, receive pass, finish.

Hockey drill B: Backwards into the circle with puck, turn, inner edge and knee / glove / elbow in the ice, repeat off blue, finish.

Hockey drill C: Inner or outer edge on a small surface with many repetitions.

Hockey drill D: Inner or outer edge and turning from backwards to forward or vice versa, on a small surface with many repetitions.

The skating drills can be carried out over the whole rink, crosswise or that the players start from a corner, pick a puck with them from the opposite corner and do the same exercise on the backward path with puck and finish with shot on goal.

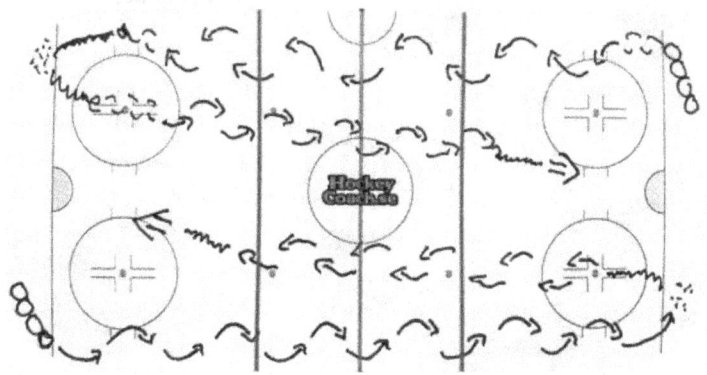

Example of doing various skating drills from two corners.

Divide the team into two corners and do for example inner edge without puck on the first leg down to the opposite corner, take puck in the opposite corner and perform the same technical step with puck and shot on goal where you started from. Use ideas for training different skills from the other drills and apply it to this set-up.

With this arrangement you get many repetitions without, and with puck, as well as many active players at the same time. The crown at work is of course that you also get a reward at the end, you get to do a shot on goal!

 Example of outer edge hockey drill over a stick, the players go an eight with the stick's help and over on inner outer edge, turns etc.

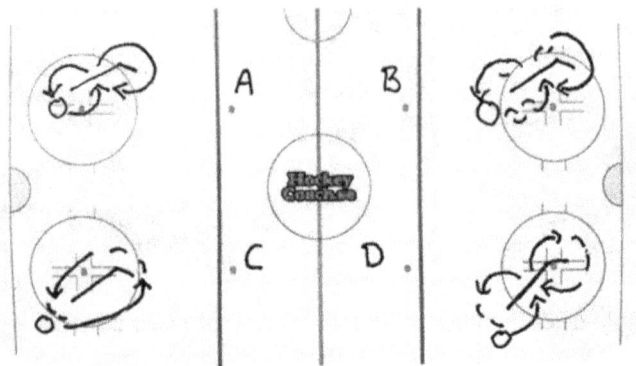

Hockey drill A: An eight round hockey stick, inner or outer edge.

Hockey drill B: An eight round hockey stick, inner or outer edge backwards.

Hockey drill C: Mohawks around the stick, raise the difficulty level by having the face in the same direction all the time, then one turn becomes extremely challenging.

Hockey drill D: Mix the Mohawks with an inner or outer edge on one foot around the stick.

You can also have the players stand still at blue- or redline and let them jump over the line, regular skate jumps, jump with the right foot (outer edge, foot closest to the line) and land on the same foot.

Some more skating drills focusing on the use of edge in the turns, forward and backwards.

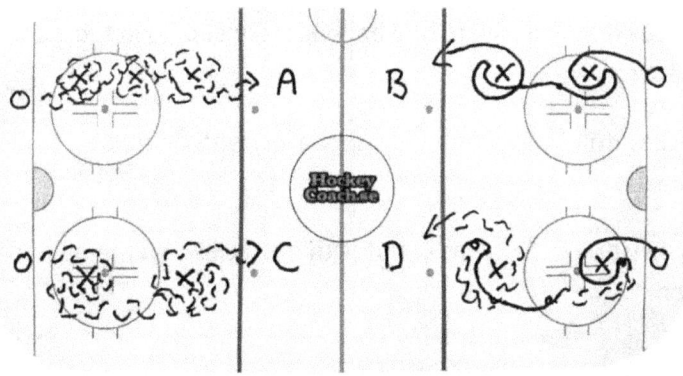

Hockey drill A: Backwards the entire lap around the cones.

Hockey drill B: Around the cone halfway forward, turn back.

Hockey drill C: Around the cone backwards halfway, turn back.

Hockey drill D: Around the cone forward halfway, turn backwards.

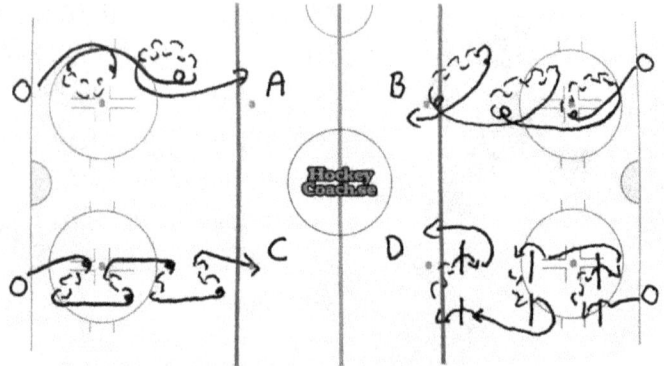

Hockey drill A: Forward and backwards in small circles.

Hockey drill B: Forward and backwards in elipses in the same direction.

Hockey drill C: Forward and backwards, with direction changes.

Hockey drill D: Same as C, but with obstacles to jump or step over.

The stride and the frequency of skating

If you simplify, you can say that three factors influence how fast a player skates, the physics, the length of the stride and the frequency.

Physics I will take as a separate part, but if we start by looking at the stride or the length of the stride, then it is quite obvious that the longer the stride is the more ice you will put under you. Long strides and glides provide a higher speed than short ones.

The third factor in fast and good skating is the frequency, that is, how quickly you get back the skate after a stride/push-off, to be able to start the next stride, under an imaginary central line from the navel and downwards, to get the maximum force in the next stride.

The physics of skating

The physics of skating is a separate area, which in turn can be divided into smaller parts, strength, mobility, speed, coordination and endurance.

Strength - This is mainly about leg strength and single-leg strength, being able to stay down in a deep skating position and make strong powerful strides.

Agility / Mobility - In order to be able to turn and be soft in skating, functional mobility is required.

Speed - Explosiveness and frequency in the first stride to be able to get up the speed, but also to maintain it.

Coordination - Changes in direction, quick turns, pivoting, and crossovers forward and backwards require body control and coordination.

Endurance - To be able to keep skating together during a whole hockey match or hockey training requires a good aerobic (with oxygen) and anaerobic (without oxygen) ability. This is about fitness, being able to both oxygenate, but also to withstand the lactic acid.

The feeling in skating

All of us are different individuals, with different bodies and physical conditions, this also provides individual skating technique. The players can remind each other, but no one goes exactly like the other, therefore, as a coach it is also possible to develop players' skating from their own comfortable skating style. Powerful but relaxed.

The skating position

The tongue on the skate should be inside the shin guards, in order to get the feeling of "hanging on the tongue". If you hang on the tongue, the angle in the knee and hip joints automatically becomes good and the player comes down in the right position.

Make sure that the players have the shin guards on the outside of the tongue, in order to be able to automatically get the right skating position, the ankle against the tongue.

An exercise to get deep down in the skating position is to push a friend in front of him (who brakes easily), or to hold both sticks and pull a friend.

Skating is of course an topic you can spend how much time you want on, but let's move on to the next capacity building block passing.

Teamwork – Capacity
- Passing

Different types of passes

The passes can be categorized into the following types, forehand pass, backhand pass, direct pass, flip pass (saucer), drop pass and board pass.

The method of practicing the various passes is to move from stationary, to motion at low speed and finally at high speed and repeat, repeat.

Example of exercise with passes in a circle with one chasing in the middle, increasing the difficulty level with two chasers, alt. two pucks. You can also control what kind of pass the players should use, forehand pass, backhand pass, direct pass or flip.

If you want to add on balance as well to the drill, you let players passing stand on two pucks.

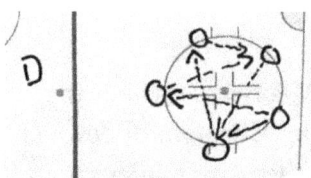

Hockey drill D: Passing in a circle standing still with 2-3 pucks, 3 pucks will be a challenge.

A couple of more passing drills on the next pages, where we move from stationary to movement.

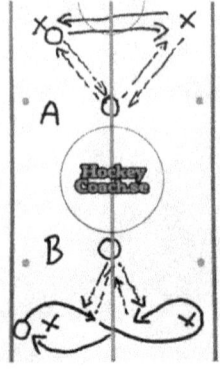

Hockey drill A: A player moves sideways, give and go passes in the extreme positions.

Hockey drill B: A player skates in an eight around the cones, give and go passes every time he is in the middle.

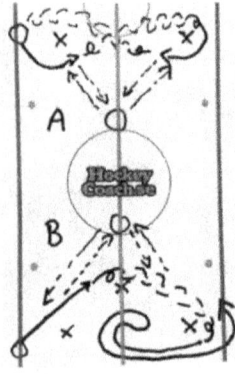

Hockey drill A: A player skates in an eight around the cones forward and backward with the chest pointing at the passer all the time, give and go passes every time player is in the middle.

Hockey drill B: Forward towards the tip of the triangle, backwards down on the other side, forward towards the starting position, turn, turn, repeat. Passes in the outside position.

...and a bit more advanced passing drill connecting to a defenseman movement on blue line.

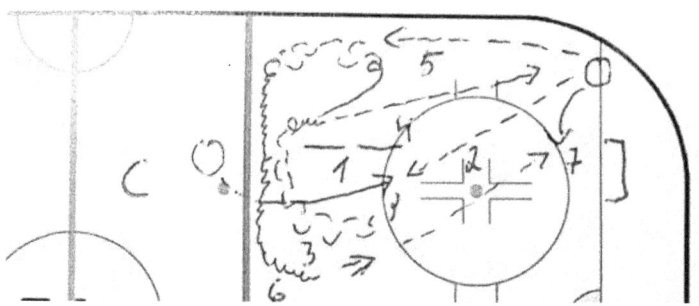

Hockey drill C 1. Down in zone 2. Receive pass 3. Bring the puck backwards around the obstacle 4. Pass the corner 5. Get back the puck 6. Enter the center for shot or shot to be steered 7. Take the role of rebound taker / to steer.

Teamwork – Capacity
- Shots

Shot from stationary, in motion and from pass

A shot can be made stationary, in motion or directly from a pass, in all three cases, the shot technique is still the same regardless of whether you shoot standing still, moving or direct shot.

Shot from stationary

The general advice and advice for shots from stationary is:

- Look up, towards the goal.

- The chest directed towards the target (not with the side forward).

- The puck on and ready at the blade (no whipping), the inside of the blade facing the target (not the blade tip).

- Weight transfer from the rear leg to the front.

- Fast and distinct arm and hand movement.

Hands and arms at shot from stationary

The general advice for shots from stationary regarding arms and hands are:

- The upper arm's elbow detached from the body
- At the shot moment, the upper arm is pulled backwards, and the lower hand / arm (power arm) pushes the hockey stick towards the ice before hitting the puck, to use the flex from the stick, which properly utilized gives a catapult similar effect.
- Turn the wrists with in the direction of the shot.
- Fast hands and arms give good shots
- Strong arms and powerful grip (grip strength) are other things needed for a good shot.

Practice shots without "treating the puck"

When you practice shots, e.g. on a shot ramp or a shot pad, be careful not to treat the puck before the shot, the puck on the blade and shoot.

Otherwise, you can practice a bad habit to "treat" the puck before the shot. See also the picture and the text of how many goals have not been done like this, to mimic and learn from after a correctly executed shot.

Shot in motion

When you shoot in motion, you should consider having the puck at 10 o'clock (22), for left shooters or at 2 (14) for right shooters, if you have the puck in this position you are always ready to shoot, but can also dribble and pass.

If you have the puck at 12 o'clock i.e. right in front of you, you already leave information to the goalkeeper, that there will not come a shot, the puck needs to be moved to shot position, before something happens. Avoid giving an advantage to the goalkeeper, send them instead information with your blade, showing that shots or passes can come at any time.

Tips on shots in motion
Some things to think about when shooting in motion beyond the tips (shots at standstill):
- Deep position (legs)
- The strength of the waist and abdomen handles the hip position at the moment of the shot.
- Arms and hip help to gain power in the shot with the center of gravity movement.
- The upper body slightly twisted but still aimed at the target.

When shooting shots on a shot ramp or a shot plate, if you have enough space, you can bring the puck forward and practice shooting in a little movement, otherwise most shots will be stationary at a shot plate.

Direct shot from a pass

When shooting direct shots from a pass, you should strive for similar technique as for shots stationary or shot in motion. If the pass becomes a little poor, you can adjust the shot position with the upper body to get a little better position.

Tips on direct shot

Some things to consider in direct shot:

- The feet in good position, deep foundation, then you have better conditions for a good shot, but also the situation immediately after the shot.

- Fast moving feet help you get right at the shot (to the puck)

- The shot position needs to be controlled throughout the execution, otherwise the shot may end up somewhere else than you wanted.

Basics in shooting technique - Weight Movement

In order to get good power in the shot, the shooting movement needs to be long and sweeping and that the whole body is used, not just the arms but also the legs, with the weight shift from the rear leg to the front.

Time limit at the shot moment

If the optimal shot comes from a long sweeping movement in the shot, then the reality is different, there is usually no time for the optimal sweeping movement at the moment of the shot, but the shot needs to come quickly, with short release time, be well placed with a short, usually a wrist movement.

Quick shots also minimize the information and time for the goalkeeper to see and understand what you are going to do or where you intend to shoot, which increases your chances of scoring.

Flex in the stick and the power forward

To be able to shoot with the right technique, the hockey stick needs to have the right hardness, softness or flex, what wording you prefer. The younger or youngest players many times have too hard/stiff sticks (too little flex or too high flex figure). A cut senior stick is not the solution.

To get the best power in the shot, the stick needs to flex. The length of the stick and the flex is most important in terms of equipment for a good shot. Today there are hockey sticks with flex starting at 16, when just couple of years ago the lowest flex was 40.

The power you produce at the actual shot must go through the stick's flex and forward, imagine that you should follow after the shot, and you will get the power forward.

To be able to utilize the flex on the stick you naturally need a flex that you master.

How long should the hockey stick be?

How long should a hockey stick be? I personally want my hockey players to have as long hockey sticks as possible. I think the hockey stick should be at least between the chin and eyes with skates on, but this is individual, rather a longer hockey stick than a short, this will

give an advantage in moving away the puck from opponent, but the longer is stick is harder to master, but if you do, you will have a big benefit.

Should the stick be too short, you can extend today's hockey sticks with a wooden knob, which costs around SEK 50 and lengthens the stick by 5-10 cm, so it is not always necessary to buy a new hockey stick just because the old hockey stick has become too short, which was the case earlier with the wooden sticks.

Why use a longer hockey stick?

If you have a longer hockey stick, then you have a longer range, which is an advantage both in attacks, defenses, shots, fakes, pass reception and close battles, provided that you master the length of the hockey stick.

A player can be fast and smooth even with a long hockey stick, in addition you get the above mentioned benefits.

In the case of shots, but also in connection with reception, the flex on the stick is important. With too soft hockey sticks, a hard pass is released under the hockey stick and a hard hockey stick can cause the puck to bounce even if you try to be soft in the reception.

Flex 16-20 for the youngest (can be found on e.g. Vikkela.com) 30-45 for the young, Flex 47-65 intermediate, and 75-100 flex for adults.

To think about: A cut stick has a different flex than the one that stands on the shaft, a 40 flex, could turn into 50 flex if you cut it a lot.

That was some theory about shots and shooting technique, now let's look at some hockey drills where the shot is in focus.

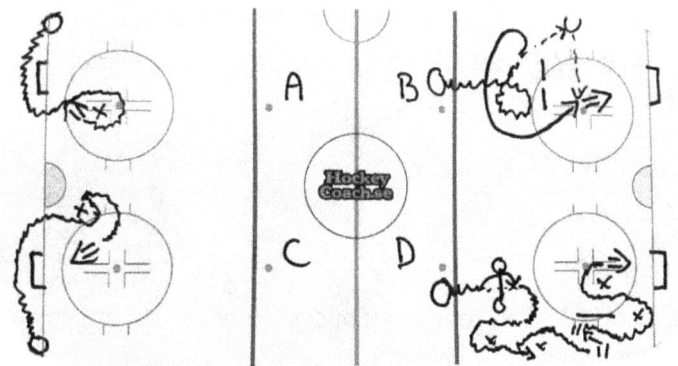

Hockey drill A: Around the goal and the cone, shoot.

Hockey drill B: Turn inside blue, fast crossovers around, pass and direct shot.

Hockey drill C: Around the goal and the cone halfway, and then back for the finish.

Hockey drill D: Jump over obstacle, against blue, around the cone, fake pass at the second cone, two stops between the cones, go for goal.

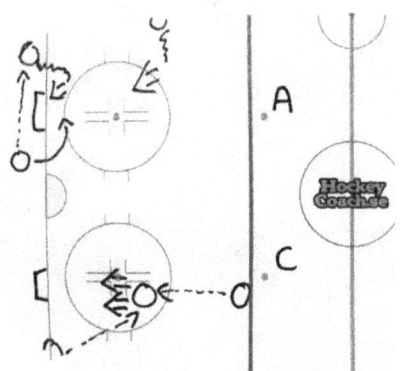

Hockey drill A: Pass behind goal, fast finish, passers in at the far post, shot from blue.

Hockey drill C: Pass from blue straight from behind to shooter, finish. Pass from corner, direct shot.

It's also very good to sometimes practice shots, where everything is not perfect, a bouncing puck, puck in air etc.

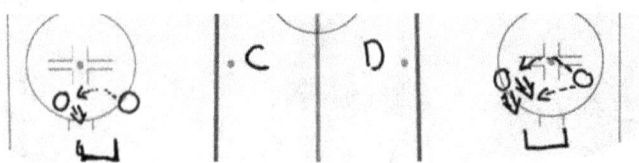

Hockey drill C: A player throws pucks in the air, the other shoots on volley.

Hockey drill D: One player throws pucks in the air, one pass along the ice, shot on volley and from the ice, in a quick sequence.

And a couple of drills combining individual skills (skating and stick handling) before the shot.

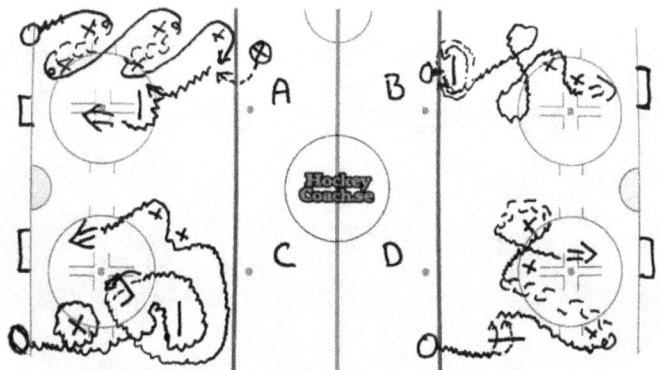

Hockey drill A: Forward and backwards around the cones with or without puck. At blue, a leader or other player throws a puck in the air, which the player takes down with his hand, makes a fake and finishes. If the exercise is started with the puck, it is passed to the player who throws the puck and then stops the pass with his feet's, while the player throws the puck to the buddy.

Hockey drill B: Long draw in a circle around an obstacle, one lap in both directions, two turns and slalom between the cones before shooting.

Hockey drill C: Full turn around the cone, change of direction and around the next obstacle, jump over obstacle, cross overs around, slalom between the cones and shot.

Hockey drill D: Straight ahead with puck, jumping sideways, forward down into corner, backwards up, forward toward goal, backwards up around the cone, forward and shoot.

Teamwork – Capacity
- Food, rest and sleep

Load, recovery and diet during exercise

The title contains three important ingredients for an athlete or elite athlete. All three parts, load, recovery and diet need to be in balance with each other, to avoid congestion, diseases and injuries.

 Then it is important to have the right perspective on the load, to train twice a week, does not require jumping over a training so that "energy level" is good for the match on Sunday, which is happening a lot in the younger age groups?

Later there will come a story about a hockey talent and upcoming hockey star, please have a look at those practice occasions and share with the parents who thinks once or twice a week is enough.

Before, during and after training and match

Being a hockey player is about thinking in a holistic view, you are not just hockey player during the training or the match.

- Rest and sleep to be able to take advantage of the training.

- Good and nutritious food throughout the day, with the right interval, good planning is of course required.

- Take care of the equipment, no surprises when going out to exercise or match

- Always warm up before, be prepared when training or match begins

- Find ways to focus for training and match

- Give everything in all situations

- Ask the leaders for tips and advice

- Analyze yourself, what went well and what can I improve for the next training or match

Very few simple advice, which shows the 24 hour perspective if you want to succeed.

Jet lag among athletic youth

Many or most serious athletic youths take care of their rest and sleep correctly during the weeks, but during the weekends when there is extra time for recovery, many players "turn around the clock" and use the nights for e.g. to play games online, this means that during the next week, when it is time to train hard again, the player suffers from a self-created jet lag, which affects the whole week's training and matches.

Regular circadian rhythm

Outside sport, circadian rhythm is one of the most important areas, together with regular food and rest. A night's bad sleep does not do so much, but a growing lack of sleep will affect the reaction ability, reflexes, memory functions and increase the risk of infection.

To be able to perform at the top and develop as an athlete, the circadian rhythm should be the same during the week's every day, one hour here or there does not hurt, but disturbances of three hours and over will affect the biological clock, in the worst case you have acquired Jet lag symptoms, except you have not travelled anywhere.

The recommended amount of sleep for young players is approx. 10 hours sleep per night.

Diet and supplements

The diet and dietary supplements are gaining more and more space both in society and in sports and the debate goes on if "ordinary food" according to the plate model suffices or if you need to shoot supplements for an athlete.

The recommendations for nutritional intake, for "normal people", cannot be equated with elite athletes. At the same time, you should probably not listen fully to eager diet supplements either.

Who is right then? Is ordinary household food enough for an athlete? Yes, if you get in it, cereal products, vegetables, berries, fruits, meat or fish, eggs, milk products and mineral-containing beverages in the right amount. Otherwise, you need to supplement with what you lack in the form of dietary supplements.

Surveys show that getting athletes succeed in getting the right amounts from the above categories, usually lacking in the category of berries and vegetables. Larger deficiencies exist in the younger, who often take the shortcut via fast food and ready meals.

A food diary can help in the analysis of the nutritional intake and the assessment if you need to support with dietary supplements, at the same time you must remember that it is about supplements, not replacement of regular food or about saving time, in order to avoid cooking.

Practices, food sleep/rest are building a players individual capacity.

The last pages has been about hockey sticks, regular sleep and good food, let's return back to the more practice related topics in the category of building up the capacity part.

Teamwork – Capacity
- Talent or a lot of practice?

Strengthen team resources and skills

Build up your resources and your players' individual skills. A team of individual skilled players obviously has better opportunities for success compared to less skilled teams. The team capacity includes physics, technical skills, fitness, speed, strength, body size, attitude, motivation, mental or psychological skills and coordination ability. Other categories include age, experience, education, gender and social status. Support around the team is also included here, as assistant coaches, goalkeeper coaches, team coaches, masseurs, doctors, sports psychologists etc.

"National captains and coaches from all over the world felt that Mourinho got the best results with less resources than his rivals." / Franz Beckenbauer

He was lucky?

They had such luck with that move or their team had more luck than we had, it was only lucky that he managed to make that last goal. Have you heard these words or sentences? I think you have heard these expressions a number of times and maybe used them yourself, I have.

But is there really luck connected to the performance, it cannot be that some are born with more luck than others?

Many times we do not reflect on what is behind the "luck", the hard work and the commitment, the more you practice and train the more "luck" you will get.

For me, it is quite obvious that there are thousands of hours of hard work, learning, studying and training. Success in your team does not happen because the stars in the sky are in the right position, success is created. Looking at the leadership model again, can that be your formula for "luck"?

Leadership responsibility				Team Responsibility	
		Teamwork			
Energy / Engagement	Direction / Goals	Capacity	+ Team Spirit	- Collaboration losesses	Results (Hard and soft)
Feedback and learning					

How important is it to practice by yourself?

The simple answer is, extremely important. This is something that every player should learn from the beginning, to automate their own training, it becomes a habit that you do without have to think about or force themselves on, the earlier you start the earlier you inherit a good habit of training yourself.

Stretching and softening of muscles can be a given evening activity in front of the TV. However, warming up and running stretching after and before a workout (20-30 minutes), should also be a natural habit.

"Is it because we have been lucky? Of course not. It is about anything but luck when you talk about my players." / José Mourinho

Practicing is my secret - 10,000 hours - 10 years

Let's talk a little bit more about individual capacity. A number of studies have shown that it takes ten thousands of hours to become a master of what you do. This applies to leadership, professional hockey players, work, hobbies etc. Each of us has the potential to master what we do, but it will take time, 10,000 hours or about ten years. The same goes for automating a movement (technical moment, a fake, shot etc.), but here we are talking about 10,000 repetitions. Therefore, you need to focus your energy if you want to be the best.

Many of us / players / leaders are not ready to go 100% into what we are doing, but we still hope to be the best or recognized, sometimes we give up too early and wonder why we never become / became the best. But the number of training hours is missing.

"I was a great talent when I was young ..." Have you ever heard it?

Talent or a lot of training?

Talent is a word we use to simplify the explanation of success in the difference between the best and the "ordinary / normal" people or the hockey players.
We also sometimes assume that elite hockey is only for people with the right legacy and genes and unfortunately we were not one of them ... that's why we are coaches or leaders?

What if it wasn't, and it can only be seen as a claim that prevents us from being the best? What happens if our success is only linked to how many hours we practice?

For example, many hockey coaches say they can find and see talent, is that true?

Or are they just good at seeing players who have already practiced more than the others?

You can have talented parents, but it is probably more realistic that the parents have also put a lot of effort into practicing once? They also have a better sense and understanding of what is required and can convey this and coach their children.

Tiger Woods, a golf talent, or is it a result of training?

Tiger Woods has been seen as the greatest talent in golf ever. If so, you must know that Tiger Woods got his first golf set before he was one year old. He had gone through his first full round of golf when he was two years. When he was five, he had already trained more than an average golfer would do throughout his career. The same goes for Messi, Beckham, Ronaldo, Forsberg, Gretzky, Crosby and the other hockey players.

"With hard work everything is possible, everyone can dream, and what you dream of, you can reach, if you are willing to work for it" / Lionel Messi

When José Mourinho arrived in Madrid, he made a comment about Christiano Ronaldo: *"He works extremely hard, it is impressive to see a player of his caliber train harder than anyone else"*

If you count the hours that the star hockey players invested in training, it would not be a surprise why they are there, where they are, best in the league. Of course, we are not just talking about hockey specific training.

"Practicing is my secret, I have always believed in, if you want to be successful you have to work for it, train and practice and practice more". / David Beckham

I'm not sure how many hours of training I can give you by reading this book, but at least some valuable time and leadership knowledge I hope.

Repeat mode

Repetition is a powerful teaching and training method, think of the 10,000 hours of training, or 10,000 repetitions.

Through repetition, a new idea will be integrated as a common thing, although it was innovative or new from the beginning.

The same goes for hockey training and skills, repeating, repeating, training and training, and your players will integrate what you have practiced into the games. We need to be reminded more often, rather than instructed? Automated movements will build up your capacity and reduce collaborative losses.

Pareto rule 20-80 can be good to keep in mind when talking about practices and training. The 20/80 rule states that, 80% of the results will come from 20% of your activities / drills / skills, in other words, the amount of different variations of fakes, for example, when you have automated a basic skill at the bottom, it is easy to "spontaneously" add a step e.g. during the match.

You can see incredible fakes and moves made by the stars in the NHL or other top leagues, and at peak speed, and we are surprised, how did they succeed with that or how could he do it? The answer is simple, by repeating and hours of practice, to automate the movements. You can only watch a hockey team while warming up and you can see many players, who do individual stick handling practices while waiting for their turn, something to include in your training, practice while you wait?

Reaching the "elite"

Reaching the elite within their sport requires sacrifices, planning, own drive and training hours, 10,000 hours. It is much easier, more fun and more motivating to gather these training hours with the help of several sports.

I have previously mentioned the five basic physical requirements for a good hockey player, coordination, speed, mobility, strength and endurance, hardly anything you only get through ice hockey? Participation in several sports is also based on the improved understanding of the game, as well as the probably so important competition experience and the competition habit.

I would probably say that it is the experience of competition situations from other sports together with your special sport that creates successful players. If you have also played spontaneous hockey on the street, it will be so good, in the long run against the elite...

Positive expectations and the amount of training

After effective, intensive training and the amount of training, encouragement and belief in success is the next success factor. In 1968, social psychologist Robert Rosenthal made a famous experiment at a school in the United States, he let the students do a talent test.

Randomly, he and some researchers selected a number of students and presented them to the teachers as the most prominent and talented (these students were just randomly picked).

Later when the students were tested for real, the students that the teachers had heard would make great progress also proved to be better.

However, other students who had also shown development were not experienced as good, by the teachers.

Expectations and believe create development, but can also prevent it if expectations are the reverse!

Belief in talent

The belief that talent are something innate is deeply rooted in many, but more and more research shows that genes have a very small, if at all, role for talent. Instead, practice, encouragement and motivation (your own drive) are lifted, as the more decisive factors.

The experiment in the 1960s, called the Rosenthale effect, shows that positive expectations can lead to good results.

With pep talk, feedback and dedication, the teachers, as they thought, got talents to perform more and they also saw their development to a greater extent.

Belief in training

Psychology professor Anders Eriksson at Florida State University has studied top or elite performances in everything from football and chess to surgery and music. His research shows that genes are not what decide if we will be successful.

Instead, it is intensive and qualitative exercise and training for 10,000 hours which make you become good, or best at what you do.

In one of his studies he studied three groups where everyone

had begun their activity when they were seven years old and initially practiced and trained about the same. From their teens, the differences began to appear, the "stars" had trained far more than everyone else, more than 10,000 hours. Group two had trained 8,000 hours and group three 4,000 hours.

Qualitative (effective and intensive) training hours in large quantity, combined with motivation and belief in success make the difference!

Another way to find talent...

Teemu Selanne talked about success and talent at his hockey camp in Vuokatti, Finland. Selanne told about a team try-out in Russia, where the legendary coach and player Tarasov would put together an elite group of ten-year-old hockey players. When the players arrived at the ice rink he made the teams outside the locker room, you enter that locker room, you go to the other and so on.

When the first sorting was finished, he told that one team will win big! An assistant coach asked how he could be so sure, he has not even seen the players on ice?

Tarasov replied, wait and see during the match, but he was completely convinced that the team he had chosen would win.

The team that Tarasov had pointed out as a winners, won the game easily, with 12-2.

How could he see the talent or skills without having seen the players on the ice or even dressed up?

So what was the secret?

The secret was that he put all the players where the mom or dad carried the hockey bag in one locker room and all the players who came and carried their own equipment themselves in the other, for the sake of clarity, this was the team that Tarasov believed in as the winners.

He looked at players own drive, motivation and engagement, players who carry their own equipment are also probably players who can also get out and practice extra themselves.

How do your players arrive? How does it look like before the training?

How did today's hockey talents get to the top?

How has todays "talents" reached the top? Everyone has, started their career early, around the age of 5 to 6 years old, they have been engaged in many sports during childhood.

In the 10-11 age group, they trained around 20-30 hours a week, where the largest amount or number of hours has come from spontaneous training.

All of them had good training opportunities, trained and played with older players, even here in the form of spontaneous sports on the street or on a nearby area/rink.

They were helped by "enthusiasts" in the club/team.

Had a strong parental support.

Had a living with orderly conditions, focusing on order and good food, sleep and priority on sports.

A hockey talent and upcoming hockey star?

There has been a lot of focus on the subject of talent and whether you have talent or whether it is actually that you train yourself to be classified as talent?

In the previous post, I wrote about how today's "talents" have reached the top and become stars. How does it look to those who are still on the journey to get there?

I saw something exceptional during Sweden Hockey Trophy a couple of years ago, a three year younger player who was the best in every match and on all levels out on the ice (except in size then), against absolute best teams from Sweden (U11)

I also got the privilege of exchanging experiences with the father for the great talent.

Some keys to success:

"He started in the hockey school when he was 3 years old, but was on skates already as a two-year-old"

"He has averaged 5 hours organized practice on ice per week from the age of 3, but he laid the foundation for everything when he got his in lines when he turned 3, as soon as he woke up he put the in lines on his feet and set up a hockey goal in the kitchen so he had something to shoot at. There he collected huge amount of hours"

"At the age of 4, he was at the "public skating" where he could average 10 hours a week, then it is just about playing for "fun" no organized practices"

"His big advantage is that he loves the sport very much and understands it, he looks a lot at hockey (TV, mobile, tablet)"

"If we take the last year, he got the school to agree he could go to the ice rink himself (schools is located right next to the ice rink) instead of being at the school in "after school activities", waiting for the parents to pick up the children, and he is going to the rink every day after the school"

You need to have aptitude for different things, but it is still your own drive (like what you do) that is number one, then it is also easy to get together the training hours.

After that you need to have training conditions, supportive parents and leaders, four areas that do difference, areas this great hockey talent seems to have in place.

Great luck wishes (I know, I have written earlier luck has nothing to do with success) on the journey towards the future, it will be fun to follow this great "talent"! I usually do not take things in advance, it is a long and hard road where much can happen, but it would be really nice to see the choices in the NHL drafts 2025 in advance ;-) (Filip Ekberg, born 2007)

"Max Domi has trained like a NHL player from the age of 14-15 until the present date." / Mats Sundin.

Something to consider when learning new skills

All practice is about, learning, strengthening and automating skills and movements. One aspect to consider when practicing technical skill or a technical part is the opposite of social loafing, social co-operation, that means that we will work better and sharpen our minds when we have people around us, who looks at us when we train and perform the steps, but there is one but, this only applies to simpler tasks or already known moments and activities that it will apply to.

When you learn or practice a new technical skill, it is better that not many people or team members look at you, it will make you/your player unnecessarily nervous, stressed and insecure. Your stress level will pass your optimal performance level and therefore the skill learning will not be the best.

So when you train a new technical part with your players, you can divide your team into small groups to lower the physical and psychological stress level and thereby gain a better learning environment. It is also easier for you to give feedback in smaller teams.

When your players are more familiar with the new technical part, you can start training in larger groups, to raise the stress / excitement level to be more in match mode. In the end, we should always train match-like.

Another aspect of skills learning is visualization.

One part of learning a new skill is of course practicing it. The other part is the mental training. The players can practice visualizing the right technique in their mind (e.g. performing a toe drag), what actually is happening when you do this, is that you create images in your brain of a successful performance and the brain actually will also send electronic signals to the right parts of your body (muscles). Amazing!

After a while you can add another aspect to this, visualizing the skill in connection with an important match (now think of an important game and how you perform the skill successfully).

If you add visualization to this type of exercise, you have a powerful tool for the future, even if the player is training alone, they can add visualization to their own routines in their spare time. They can visualize one against one situation in the cup final, where they pick up their "signature fake" and perform it successfully.

When you at one point are in that situation for real (the cup final) the player's brain have already "been there, and done it" and it becomes a little easier to perform well and to have a lower stress level compared to, no mental training.

Teamwork – Capacity
- Efficient and Intensive hockey practices

Effective hockey training

How active are the players during a hockey training? How much active time does a player have during a 60 minute practice?

Studies that have been done and my own evaluations with the tool that I have created, to measure the efficiency and number of repetitions on a training (you find it on HockeyCoach.se), show that players in U9 - U15 team are active between 8 and 30 minutes on a hockey training. The average is somewhere around 15-25 minutes on a 60 minute hockey training, scary?

Actually, I think it's a bit scary if a player queues, waits, sits in the booth or leans towards the board for 35 - 45 minutes and is active for 15-25 minutes on the training. (A deep dive in this topic in the book "Multidimensional hockey drills and training")

It is of course not possible to be active for 60 minutes at a high intensity level, but efficiency can be increased, right? How does your hockey training look like, how active are the players?

How to increase the efficiency of the hockey training?

If the activity is only between 8 minutes at least and 15-25 minutes on average for a 60 minute hockey training, what is behind it? Some things that drive the waste of ice time are, of course, too few players active at the same time on the ice.

Another time "eater" is the transition between the hockey exercises, briefings, movement of pucks and water breaks. Other things are poor planning, unprepared leaders and players, unclear roles on the ice, poor discipline among the players etc.

If you turn it over, what can you do to streamline your hockey training?

- Plan the training

- Review of the training and hockey drills before the training

- Focus and presence during training

- Clear roles between the leaders during the training, who does what and when

- Move away some of the reviews / feedback on the ice to after the training in the locker room

- Create routines for the transitions between exercises for both players and leaders, who does what, when you blow the whistle?

- Analyze your own training with the help of the tool available on the page or a video recording

Even if you eliminate "waste time" from the exercise and increase the active part, you also have to look at the intensity during the hockey exercises in parallel. Do the players give everything, do they go with full intensity, and do they push themselves to develop?

Increase the intensity of the hockey training

One thing is to minimize the waste time during the hockey training, to increase the effective and active time, the second aspect is to increase the intensity during the training.

Hockey is played 5 against 5, or 1 against 1 (X 5) which probably a math teacher would have said. Basically, it is about winning your fight against an opponent to create a 2 against 1 situation in order to gain an advantage and be able to score goals.

It is the 1 against 1 situation that is the key in the training, creating battle and competition and thereby increasing the intensity. The basics of the technique/skills should be taught in calm environment and really with few "spectators" as possible, but then the intensity needs to be stepped up, via battle and competition.

Load and rest during exercise

During a training, recovery is also needed, which is achieved with variation in the load level between the station drills / exercises and with the regulation of the number of players per station.

If you want to have a relationship, such as work one, rest three (this equals to the workload during a hockey game with three lines). In that case it is easiest to have four players per station (one doing the drill). If instead two are running at the same time, you must have eight players (two active at the same time) or 12 players, if 3 players are activated in one station / drill, to automatically get the right relationship between activity and rest, in this example work one, rest three.

Most times work one, rest one is a good model or mindset.

Teamwork – Capacity
- Small Improvements

Skate the extra strides

I mentioned earlier that the capacity part is the easiest part to copy between different teams or at least parts of it.

If you assume that the team at a certain level is practicing and training just as much as your team every week, let's say four times a week.

Of course you want to be better than your opponents, then there are some options, you can choose to increase the number of practices or work to improve the quality of your exercises, in order to "stay ahead" the other teams.

Let's take a theoretical example, 4 (exercises) x 31 (weeks, length of season) = 124 training sessions in a season. Each exercise contains 5 exercises, 5 x 124 = 620 exercises. Each exercise is repeated 10 times per player during the training, 10 x 620 = 6200 repetitions.

During these exercises, players will step into the drill many times and glide instead of skate with full speed and powerful strides, e.g. in the beginning or at the end of the drill, or when returning to the starting point.

Instead of increasing the amount of training sessions, you can insert small focus areas, "Enter all drills with three quick and fast strides", go the last three meters or go three meters after a drill (e.g. back check). 3 meters extra for each drill and repetition, this would mean 6200 reps X 3 meters X 20 players = 372,000 meters. Your team would, with this little improvement, skate 372 kilometers extra during the season, the result, increased capacity, should be visible at the end of the matches or at the end of the season. You should have physically and mentally strong players, they will take the extra strides needed to succeed.

In combination with the skating and the intensity of the training, you can also let your players train for example, a fake/stick handling while waiting. 10000 reps will automate the movement, 10,000 hours will make you the master of it and reduce the team's collaborative losses!

What own ideas do you have to streamline and improve your practices? How can you use or reduce the "waste time"?

Theoretically a player doesn't need to drink water during a 60 practice...

The power in small steps

You can of course use the same principle for improvements in general or your work towards a common goals. Let's say you can make 3 small improvement steps every day, after a month you have 90 small improvement steps and after 6 months 540. If you can get each player in your team to take these small improvement steps you have 540 X 20 players = 10800 small improvements in your hockey team. This can be an individual challenge for every practice for your players, which three things can you do better today than during the previous training?

Other good questions in the dialogue about the players' development can be: What do you think you have to do to reach your short-term goal? How can you do it yourself? What activities can you do yourself? How often? When? How can you do it in a fun way that motivates yourself?

"We think of the brain as a repository to be filled when we should think of it as an instrument to be used." / John W Gardner

Continuous hockey improvements

The hockey is a complex sport with many game and technical moments to master, there are many areas to develop, both small and large, on and off ice. Therefore, it constantly needs to be analyzed from the coaching team how the game and training can be developed.

Being a youth leader today is not the same as 10 years ago not even 5 years ago. The best thing is of course if you can stand for the development yourself, or look at what others are doing, it is many times said that the copy never gets better than the original, but to merge two copies (new thinking) will probably be.

There is rarely anyone revolutionizing the training or matches, but gathering good smaller ideas from others and creating and connecting a larger picture of those pieces, can be something good and new.

The holistic view/ whole picture / connected picture is for me keywords, I get allergic when you just focus on parts of things

and pick them in, it works if you know how it affects the full picture, but usually this is missing, you copy something, not just in ice hockey, but don't understand the purpose.

Hard practice or have fun?

The hockey training of the children and young people should be based on fun and competition according to me both on and off-ice, here I think you often only hear the word fun, but the competition part gives it an extra spice. Most players want to develop and test their strength and capability against others and having fun on the road means of course not that you do not do things properly or practice the technique correctly, which is sometimes also forgotten.

"If you have too much fun on the practice, you will not have so much fun on the match"

"Fun hockey exercises"

I think fun hockey exercises or practices is one of the most Googled hockey training word combinations. In order to get fun hockey exercises and hockey training, I think that as a

basic idea you should have a long-term perspective and versatility in the back of the head.

Give players the opportunity to be active and in motion, avoiding queuing and waiting. Game and competition moments in the exercises puts an extra spice to get into fun hockey exercises.

... This situation can only occur nowadays during the first training in the hockey school, before we have corrected the "error"? But it is a really good example of a man against man defense?

Sports teacher vs. Swedish Language Teachers

Speaking of building capacity, I heard the following from Claes Hellgren (physics coach in Hammarby Football and former national team goalkeeper in handball, as well as sports teacher)

"A sports teacher's result is that 70% of the previous students are inactive at the age of 30! Lucky that the Swedish language teacher does not have the same track record? "

...Talking about building capacity.

Teamwork Team-spirit

Leadership responsibility					Team Responsibility
		Teamwork			
Energy / Engagement	Direction / Goals	Capacity	+ Team Spirit	- Collaboration losesses	Results (Hard and soft)
Feedback and learning					

The next part of the teamwork block is the team spirit, it is of course also a part you should try to strengthen.

Team spirit can be described in many different ways, here are some keywords and sentences:

- How well we know each other
- To strive for a common goal
- Commitment to accomplish something together
- Clarity in roles
- Pride to belong to the team
- Satisfaction from performance
- Honesty in the group
- Loyalty in the team
- Positive communication and feeling in the group
- Humility, we are just as much worth everyone in the team
- We are ready to make sacrifices for others in the team
- Solves problems together
- Good communication
- Supports each other
- Ethics
- Moral
- Common values and norms
- 1 + 1 = 3, together we are stronger

"I always talk like that, and I think it's important, but they believe that before I even talk to them," Berube said. "They believe that. They know if they play the right way and they do things properly and put the team first and play the team game, we're a good team." /Craig Berube

Team spirit within the team

The first thing that affects the team spirit is the size of the group. The size of the team will have a great impact on the team spirit, it is more difficult to get a good team spirit in bigger teams, not impossible, just more difficult.

In teams with good team spirit, the group members also tend to take greater responsibility for the negative results.
The team spirit will also likely increase if your players make great efforts during training or sacrifices during a match.

Improved or increased team spirit will also lead to better attendance at training and more "fighting spirit" from the players to the team during the matches, they will also have easier to respect the team's norms or rules, such as getting on time.

The level of team spirit will also affect the requested leadership style or behavior from the leaders. In many teams with lower team spirit, you can see a leadership that is more task-oriented (lower team spirit) and in the teams with better team spirit, the leadership is more relations oriented (higher team spirit). This does not mean that the leader ignores the results even if the leader is more relationship oriented and sees each individual in the team, it is rather the key to the results and not the other way around.

As said, high team spirit is usually linked to more democratic leadership. However, the feeling for team spirit can vary depending on the "status" and the results for the team. Players in the starting formation tend to feel higher team spirit than "substitutes" in a losing team, but in a successful team the difference is less visible between "substitutes" and "regular".

In addition to clear common goals, communication and roles within the team, there are some additional things to consider when it comes to building up team spirit.
- Pride for the team and what the team does, highlight it via communication or visualize e.g. newspaper articles, pictures etc.
- Team identity that starts with the match and training clothes.
- Changing rooms or other premises (e.g. storage room) connected to the team.

- Other things, accessories or symbols that will connect your players. (Water bottles, clothes, caps etc.)

To the left a wrist band, I have personally used the wrist band during some select team tournaments. It creates team feeling and unity, reminds the players of our focus, "Be a Hockey Star" on and off ice, in all situations. The wristbands can be found on:
http://hockey87.com/?product=armband-yolo-be-a-hockey-star

Avoid subgroups in the team, try to get all your players to know each other, this can be done by solving tasks together or regularly having team spirit theme and different team building activities. How the players sit in the locker room also has a big impact, are the same players always sitting next to each other?

If you know each other well and can "hang around" with everyone, it is also more likely that you will help and support each other to greater extend, in various situations.

When you really help or support others, they will do the same for you. When your players are there for each other, they will support each other, no matter what.

One of the players supporting another will next time get genuine support back. It is somehow built into our system, if you get support or get something, you want to give something back. You show respect and you get respect back. You show appreciation and you get appreciation, you help and you get help back.

Try to transfer or use this thinking and acting in your team. Show respect and you become respectful. You show appreciation and you get appreciation, you help and you get help back.

Team size

Research shows that, depending on the sport, the size of the ideal number of team members varies between sports. One common rule for good number of team members is that you should be able to play a match on your training (two teams) with limited amount of substitutes (e.g. two+ lines in each team).

In all sports, the participants felt that the team was too large or too small if the number of team members was increased or decreased by 25% compared to the first "rule".

The size of the team will also affect your and your team's ability to build the team spirit. It is easier to focus on the task in small teams, but social cooperation becomes larger in larger groups, but reduces the task focus and also gives greater amount of "social loafing" (I can hide in the crowd).

Your team size will also affect the communication, it is more difficult to know the players in depth and give feedback to everyone, which also affects the team spirit. And as a result, the leadership in larger teams with greater number of players in the team, tends to be less democratic.

The bigger the dream, the more important the team is. A leader never gets more results than the team will deliver.

Creating team spirit

Good team spirit creates a winning climate, good team morale and faith in the team's success, and players will make more sacrifices for the team and work harder for success.

Group dynamics

So far, I have talked about Steiner's model in the teamwork section, but of course there are other models that can help you understand your team's behavior and development.

Below is a summary of Tuckman & Jensen, 1977, team development model.

Forming - The group members get to know each other and begin to identify the task / challenge they face and how to solve it. This is a very exciting phase for every team member, even though they may have spent one or more seasons together, but when you add or remove players or change the goal of the team, you start from the beginning by forming the group.

Storming - Now the "honeymoon" is over and you will probably or more likely to face conflicts and tensions in your team, between the players and sometimes between you and one or several players (or it will be hidden under the surface, for you). The conflict can be about the roles in the team, behavior, norms, tactics etc. If the conflicts are not handled, the team will not take the next step in the team development and instead get stuck in this phase, which many groups do or commute between the first and second steps.

Norming - Players begin to find their places and roles within the team. Roles and norms are becoming established and clear to everyone, both in terms of the task, the cooperation and the work morale within the team. The goals become clearer and clearer and the cooperation is strengthened within the team.

Performing - Now the team is "ready", relationships, roles, goals and norms are clear to everyone and accepted. The focus is now on the first steps towards the common goal in the short and long term (performance together).

Adjourning - The season is over and the motivation is lower than before and the relationship between the players may not be so important anymore, the focus begins to shift towards holiday and the next season's challenges.

To take the group further in the various steps, the leadership model is the first tool, but also various team building exercises help, look at the next step and find the answer for what needs to be in place (e.g. step 1 – know each other), in order to use the correct teambuilding activities, later you will find a number of suggestions for different team building exercises that will strengthen the team spirit, but in many cases also other areas in the leadership model.

Home and away matches - unbeaten at home

Other aspects that may affect the team spirit are at home and away matches. You can talk about three different levels of "territories", primary, secondary and public.

In the primary area, the team has full control and other people are not allowed (or only have very limited access) in this zone, it can be the team's own premises and other facilities. This zone is often designed, colored and "decorated" with important symbols or images to enhance the team and also the club spirit. The greater the control the team has in its primary territory, the more they are willing to "protect" it.

In the secondary area, the team has some control, but the facilities can also be used by others, training facilities can be shared with other teams within the club, or by other associations e.g. figure skating.

In the third territory or in the public area, you can count in public educational facilities and also facilities at away games. In away games, the visiting team will be placed in a non-personal dressing room.

Create a winning climate

You can have capacity, talent and ability, but if there is a lack of faith, there will be a lack of results. In this case, the most valuable tool is for you in your leadership feedback. Make sure you create the images of success and faith inside the players' heads.

José Mourinho works with each player's self-image, although he may have many of the best football players in the world. They still need to be seen, feel the confidence and faith of their coach. How you see them is how they see themselves as players.

Here are some practical tips on how to create a winning climate and winning roles within your team.

- Create a list of strengths for each player in the team and focus on talking about these with your players.

- Notice your own attitude towards the players, try to "zero" that from time to time and focus on the positive things.

- Talk about each player's strengths, show them you believe in them.

- Expect the best of each player, show it through communication and action.

Players want to exceed expectations (yours and others), they want to be winners, you can help them, show it through your communication and actions!

"A loser gets bitter when he is behind and unclear when he is ahead"

"A winner keeps his faith and balance, regardless of his position"

"Being afraid of losing, takes away the will to win"

We are a team

The statement "The first liner / first line will not be a correct word. I need you all. You need each other. We are a team. " Shows how important José Mourinho sees each player in his team.

In order not to be eaten up in competition with other teams and unhealthy competition internally within the team, he creates a culture where everyone knows and feels that they are an important part of the team puzzle. Each player must act as a leader regardless of rank or position within the team, with this I mean that the players take responsibility for their own role, results and thus also for the team's results, they are leaders from their position, during training, match and outside the hockey. Every player is part of the management team within the team, no matter if it it's a small role!

With this vision everyone must show "leadership", take responsibility for the results, inspire teammates and therefore also act positively towards their teammates, be, and show that they are leaders regardless of position within the team, defense, forward, goalkeeper or "waterboy". The same applies regardless of age, life experience, or social status, you have the power to show leadership, no one can remove it from you if you decide to do so. Make your players aware of this, this is what Mourinho is doing.

"For example, I love Geremi on the bench, because he is a low-profile player ready to help, ready to fight for the team, ready to do the job, the job I want him to do." / José Mourinho

"Why drive Aston Martin all the time, when I have Ferrari and Porsche too? It would just be stupid" / José Mourinho

Enemy outside the team?

The best way is, of course, to build on the team spirit in a constructive way within your own team and with a focus on the own team, however, it has turned out that the team spirit within the team will in most cases also increase when you have another team to compete against or a common "enemy" outside the team, here you can discuss the moral in it...

However, this is something that Mourinho uses systematically, creates enemies outside the team, to make the team stronger from the inside.

"I knew it would happen a long time ago, but I don't care. I know because I know who controls the game, and if you look at their statements, then you understand why they have made this decision play Saturday night at 22:00, then on a Tuesday in the Champions League. Barcelona does not want to play on Saturday because they are playing on Wednesday before, and because of this we have to play on a Monday. "

As a leader, you have to take responsibility for the extreme situations and the we vs them thinking, which can happen in sport. A joint fight against an "enemy" outside the team will strengthen the team spirit, but in the long term may create an unhealthy hostility towards other groups or teams and it should not be necessary to do this especially in youth teams.

You should focus on the challenge or compete against the situation instead of an enemy outside the team, I just wanted also to address this more "primitive" aspect of building team spirit.

Teamwork Team-spirit
- Clear roles

Each role is an important role ... Role definitions

In general, you can say that a role is the behavior expected of an individual in a particular situation or position. You can split roles into two categories, formal and informal roles. The formal roles are defined and accepted by the team, defensive player, forward, goalkeeper, team captain etc. The informal roles will develop within the team when the players get to know each other. Some of the informal roles can be the "informal leader", "the clown", "socialist", "the driving force" etc.

A role is built up by expectations

A role in a team consists of four parts.
- Coaches and other leaders' expectations on the player
- Other team members' expectations on the player
- Other people's expectations on the player
- The player's own expectations, needs and resources
All these four parts will form the player's role, how the player has interpreted the expectations and what he / she believes he must live up to and accept in the role.

Two role aspects will affect the player's performance

Clarity - How clear is the content and the expectations of the player's role? How clear are responsibilities and authority in this role?

Approval - Is the player willing to accept the role completely? Will this role provide enough satisfaction for the player so that he / she continues to be motivated? It can be about being able to use special skills and capacity to the fullest, but it can also be about how important the role is to the team's success or how much attention or feedback you get from coaches other leaders and fellow players.

These two aspects, clarity and acceptance or approval of the role, will constitute the player's role performance.
If you add an additional dimension to it, you can talk about individual roles in the collective team (the role in the team or the role for the team).

"If you have a Bentley and an Aston Martin, but you only go with Bentley every day and leave Aston Martin in the garage, you're a little stupid."
/ José Mourinho, defends his player rotation

A Winning Role - You Can Do It!

As I wrote earlier, expectations create roles, here I will give you the definition of a role once again.

A role within a team consists of four parts.

- The coach and other leaders' expectations on the player

- Other team members' expectations on the player

- Other people's expectations on the player

- The player's own expectations, needs and resources

These four parts will form the player's role, how the player has interpreted the expectations and what he / she believes he must live up to and accept.

Normally, we only associate the role with the position a player has in the team, forward, defender or goalkeeper, but can this be used in a creative positive way? Can it be used to create a winning role?

If part of the role is about expectations from coaches and leaders, then your expectations, communication and feedback will be important in creating the "winning role".

Show in practice that you believe in each individual, show them you think they can be the best, think and show you believe they can do it ... obviously with synchronized video and audio (body language and word selection).

Here it's important to balance the beliefs / positive expectations vs feeling of pressure, you do not want to cross the line to the pressure side, so the player feels a pressure that he / she has difficulty accepting (I must succeed, they leader has so high expectations on me).

I believe you can do it, or the winning role, which I describe, does not have to be about winning matches, it is about believing in the possibility of success and development, which of course will ultimately be reflected in the results. (YOU / WE CAN DO IT).

Waterboy example, you can do it...

http://youtu.be/Nwv61Uu1fdA

...And Barack Obama's example you can do it, yes we can.

http://youtu.be/47MKGOPP4Zo

I'm not in politics, but Obama's short speech is pretty impressive? Talk about creating positive expectations, you can do it!

The "I" in the Team or "I" for the Team

The individual I-part is incredibly important, but must fit into the team.

Everyone chooses how they want to look at things, and also how they react to them! Each player chooses their own thinking, reactions to things, for example, you become provoked or you ignore things, it's your own decision. This applies also for how a player see their own role, what decisions they will take and how they will act in a role.

Visualize this thinking for your players, they are managers of their own thinking, activities and reactions. Use basketball and the sour lemon example when you convey this message, we think right we act right! Even if something is annoying or provocative, it is ultimately we ourselves who choose the reaction.

One of my personal strongest lessons on this subject comes from the Finnish military, we were out in the woods and would place our haubits at the designated location, but when we would dig down the support legs in the ground for a haubits (cannon) and discovered that it was just big stones in the ground there, we complained to the commanders that it was not possible and that we should get a new place, but the commander simply said that it is just a little "vojvoj" (sad for you or sorry for you), but this is the position, and in the end we always got the haubits in place (sweat, some blood drops and help from a truck to pull away stones). The same answer was always given to difficult or "impossible" tasks, in the end you begin to notice that things that you have previously complained about and reacted heavily on and felt as hard, are actually not worth complaining about, it is just a little "vojvoj" and so you solve it with a smile or an internal joke about the subject.

Be the best in what you do, every day in your role. Always do your best in your role every day, tomorrow you can have a different role, but the same goes for it as well.

Individual roles need clarity and acceptance among each player in order to achieve good team performance and reduce co-operation losses.

"You have to make every player feel valuable, but not that they are irreplaceable" / Marcello Lippi

"If a person has the role of being a street cleaner, that person should sweep the streets like Michelangelo painted, or Beethoven composed music, or Shakespeare wrote poetry. He should sweep the streets so well that all the hosts of heaven and earth pause to say, here lived a great street cleaner who did his job well "/ Dr. Martin Luther King Jr.

Role Conflicts

Role conflicts can occur when expectations are not sufficiently clear or a player does not accept a role. Then you have to know that 90% of the conflicts within groups and teams are due to misunderstandings (poor communication).

Most misunderstandings occur when you are not communicating sufficiently clearly or ensuring that both parties have the same picture. Check with questions so that the individual players and the whole team have the same picture about different roles in the team.

There are no "dead ends" roles, positions or jobs, just "dead end" thinking. It is about communication about the purpose of the role, are you a stonemason or do you see that you contribute to the process of powerful stone buildings are built? This way of thinking is important to get to your players. Create clarity in the role and give it a value and purpose.

Conflict management - Relationship vs. Performance / Results

Role conflicts can be categorized into both team spirit and collaboration losses, I have now entered it into the team spirit, but it would fit just as well into the block of collaboration losses.

It is easy to sacrifice relationships, when you are just searching for results, this applies also to conflict management. First, we may need to define what a conflict is.

What different people and players regard as conflict will be very different. The short and best generic definition is when someone does not <u>accept</u> a situation, an overrun, a repetitive act or a role.

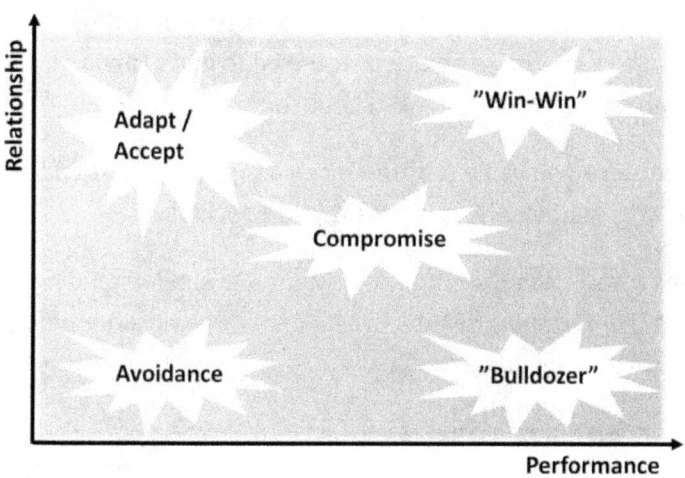

If we look at some different ways to solve a conflict, we have on the Y-scale relationship, and on the X-scale performance or results. Depending on the size of the conflict or if you value the relationship or the result, there are different ways of resolving a conflict.

Avoidance - If there is a minor conflict, your players will forget it soon and it will not affect the outcome or the relationship, even if you do not grab and handle the "conflict". "Swipe it under the mat"

Adapt / Accept - You value the relationship higher than the result and agree to adapt and give the other party right.

Compromise - Lose - Lose the situation, none of the parties in the conflict will get their desired solution and have to give up something. Example: Person X wants A, while person Y wants B, but in a compromise, the solution will be C...

Or one person wants to go to Estonia another to Lithuania, but at a compromise solution would be to go to Latvia, the country between Estonia and Lithuania...

Bulldozer - You value performance and results higher and are ready to sacrifice the relationship, you decide!

Consensus - Win-Win situation, was it a misunderstanding from the beginning? Find a way to get a win-win situation by steering the dialogue.

Misunderstanding creates conflicts

One consequence of poor listening is conflicts. Like I already mentioned over 90% of all conflicts start with a misunderstanding, we did not listen to the sender or the opposite and we did not ensure that we had the same picture with any questions, have I understood you correctly if I interpret what you said like this ... We can still have different opinions on the issue or problem, but we are aware of it at least.

Teamwork Team-spirit
- Communication

Do we use the same system?

Think of the 2-2-1 hockey system, how would you describe it? Depending on your age, geographical location, values, knowledge, skills, experience and so on, you describe it in a certain way. Do you think you and I would have the same picture?

If you were at a seminar with 100 other hockey coaches you can probably find someone with similar mindset, but otherwise you would get many different opinions about 2-2-1, ranging from extremely defensive to extremely offensive and everything in between. So if you were to attend a seminar like this and had the opportunity to talk about 2-2-1 with everyone, you would have to be really present in your listening and checking with questions that you and those who listened to you have understood correctly. The same applies to your players, you probably have much more in-depth knowledge and skills in the area and therefore have to put extra effort into creating the understanding of the message that you convey.

But what a fantastic opportunity for learning and exchanging experiences it would be, or source of conflicts (same subject, but different images = misunderstanding = conflict)

Consider the following situation. You have the responsibility to lead a hockey team and explain to the team that you want to use 2-2-1 system, and then immediately get the answer, "well we know that system, it's the same as our previous coach used". This can be a big pitfall if you think you and your players and the previous coach had the same picture of how to play 2-2-1.

Instead, you can start asking questions to understand how they played, generally, aggressively, defensively, and find similarities to your thinking, but you would also find differences in both why, what and how. By asking questions you avoid many conflicts, misunderstandings and negative feedback.

See you or send me an email?

Another part that will affect our communication is how you perceive things around you. By seeing, hearing, feeling, tasting or smelling? How do you perceive things?

If you do not have the answer you can think of how to say goodbye or end a phone call, or you might be a person who just send text messages (SMS and emails)? This will tell us a little bit about how we also want receive communication, verbally, in text or through pictures.

Personally, I usually end a meeting with "Bye, see you" (even if it is a phone call and even if I know that the next contact is made by phone). I want to see and hear things. So why do I write about this?

Because it is a very important part of the communication to reach your players with your message. I like to talk in pictures, I try to create a picture of my message at least in my leadership role, but I also therefore risk losing some of my audience, who do not understand things visually, that's why it is important to try to mix your message (See - hear - feel), pictures, written text and the possibility try out / do in practice.

If it is a large team / group you are trying to reach, combine these different methods as much as possible to reach out to the different individuals with your message. When we talk about your players, you need to try to customize your message to the individual recipient, in order to do that, you obviously need to know your players well, how do they prefer to receive information (oral communication, text or images).

For example, when you explain a drill, you can think about how you draw on the board and what instructions you convey verbally, maybe you also need to write some keywords on the board.

Set the communication frequency

When we talk about communication, we often talk about the sender and the recipient, and if it were only about these two roles, the communication would be easier. But communication takes time and has more aspects to consider, you have the skills, experience, expectations and the environment that can affect your communication.

If you have great expertise and experience in a subject, it will probably affect how you express yourself and depending on the recipient's competence and experience, your message will be interpreted in different ways.

The recipient will also be affected by his / her expectations of your message and can sometimes also turn off in certain situations, because he / she knows what is coming, now I will get some complaints again….

The environment will of course affect the understanding of your message. During a match there may be loud noice from the audience / parents that interfere with the communication and sometimes may even give opposite directives to individual players. Here communication is just as important with that group, explain what you want and your expectations on them during match and training.

Teamwork Team-spirit
- Attitude

Right Attitude = Success?

Motivation and attitude to hockey training or match is crucial for success, for example you can rarely (if ever) change the external conditions before a match or exercise, soft / hard ice, cold / warm, a long journey to away game, late / early match start, big or small ice rink etc. but you can change / influence your mental state and attitude about how you handle these situations, you can learn to accept and handle the situation and see it as a strength for yourself or for the whole team, it can be a "vojvoj situation" (provided that the other teammates can also handle the situation in this way). How can you, as a leader, contribute in this way of thinking?

(Talent + ability) X motivation / attitude = Individual performance

The teamwork block can be supplemented with another model, a model of what affects individual performance.

The model describes the importance of having a good attitude in sports / hockey / work etc. On a scale of 1 to 5, but you can of course use a scale of 1-10 if you feel more comfortable with it, but I use 1 to 5 scale in this example.

In this model for individual achievement, you value three areas, talent (capacity), ability (to use the skills) and attitude. Based on a formula, these three together create a theoretical performance result for the individual, you can also use it on team level.

I will try to translate this into two examples, two different players and then it could look like this:

The first hockey player has a little more talent (capacity) than the average (valued at a 4), he / she also has a little more ability / competence to solve the task (4), but the attitude / motivation fails and is below average (2).

In example two, we have an average good player with talent / capacity valued at (3) and skill or ability (3), but this player always has good attitude and motivation (5), regardless of situation or circumstances.

Transferring the scores for the players into the formula **(Talent + ability) X motivation / attitude = Individual performance** would give below theorethical individual performance

Player 1: (4 + 4) x 2 = 16
Player 2: (3 + 3) x 5 = 30

With these results, it would be obvious who would win the match, but this is for individual performance, but linked to Steiner's model you can still work with it in a practical way. A team made up of individually motivated players, can beat a skilled team with motivational problems at all levels. Make sure you don't lose at least because of bad attitude!

"When you play against another team with the same qualities as you, normally the best wins." / José Mourinho ... If it wasn't for the attitude / motivational part.

"Talent is not enough"

You or your players can have all the talent in the world or the best plans and goals to reach them (direction), but if you don't have energy and commitment (why should I do something, what's in it for me, see the chapters of energy), nothing will be done or it will not be done in the best way.

José Mourinho openly complained about Karim Benzema's attitude, during Real Madrid's pre-season camp in the US. Mourinho said the 22-year-old striker had to improve.

"Benzema needs to understand that he is extremely talented, but it is not enough. I need Karim. For me it is important that the players throw themselves out. We need a striker who glows, not one who is completely without energy" / José Mourinho

"Remember what I said, this is an individual sport. Every player must take care of their own tasks if the team is to succeed" / Swedish hockey coach

"You have to remember that a team consists of individuals who cooperate with each other. The team will only exist if the cooperation works well between the individuals" / Swedish hockey coach

Give 100%

Many times the expression is heard that we should give one hundred percent or more, but it tends to be a little clumsy if you are not familiar with the various parts that need to be in place. We need to understand why, we must have a clear direction on the energy and the different parts of the teamwork module need to work painlessly with small collaboration losses.

What gives 100%? Here is a small mathematical formula that can help you answer these questions:

If:

A B C D E F G H I J K L M N O P Q R S T V W X Y Z

Is represented as:

1 2 3 4 5 6 7 8 9 10 11 12 13 14 15 16 17 18 19 20 21 22 23 24 25 26

So it means:

HARD WORK

$8 + 1 + 18 + 4 + 23 + 15 + 18 + 11 = 98\%$

and

KNOWLEDGE

$11 + 14 + 15 + 23 + 12 + 5 + 4 + 7 + 5 = 96\%$

but

ATTITUDE

$1 + 20 + 20 + 9 + 20 + 21 + 4 + 5 = 100\%$

This connects quite well to the example with (Talent + ability) X motivation / attitude = Individual achievement

If you instead talk about giving more than 100%? What does it really mean to give more than 100%? We have all been on trainings, matches or meetings where someone wants you to give over 100%. How about achieving 103%?

BULLSHIT

$2 + 21 + 12 + 12 + 19 + 8 + 9 + 20 = 103\%$

And if we should reach higher than that ...

A-S-S-K-I-S-S-I-N-G

$1 + 19 + 19 + 11 + 9 + 19 + 19 + 9 + 14 + 7 = 118\%$

If the numbers match mathematical security, we can say that: Hard Work and Knowledge will get you close to 100%, and Attitude will take you there!

If we are over 100%, we are talking about Bullshit and Ass Kissing.

Teamwork Team-spirit - Teambuilding exercises

Get to know each other - Team building exercise

How: Put together a form that players can fill out.

Include things like (choose some, do not use all):

Name, age, born in (city), live, position in the team, preferably play (if I myself choose), therefore I play ice hockey, favorite team, dream of the future, hobbies, favorite programs in TV, I am good at, this I can develop, a good teammate is… (Describe behavior), thing you do not against a teammate, goals for this year's season, I like / do not like in the school / work, if I had ten million…, I, I have always dreamed of…

When the players are ready they can present what they have written in pairs / in smaller groups / for the whole group, it is important that everyone in some way hear all the presentations. Also point out that you do not laugh or ridicule someone's presentation.

To discuss:

How did you feel to tell about yourself?

How was it to hear the others' presentations?

Did it come up much that you didn't already know?

Was there a "WOW-moment" / surprise?

Create role definitions - Team building exercise

How: You can start with a theory review on how you as a leader think and expect your players to act in their different roles on the ice.

Define key points: How does a center forward act in the defensive zone / neutral zone / attack zone.

Then divide the players into groups with centers, forwards and defensive players (incl. goalies).

Their task now is to write down a "role description" for the group they belong to based on the expectations or the description you have given as introduction.

When the players are ready, they present their work to the others.

To discuss:

Have you got everything in the descriptions?

How do you do if a player changes position?

Are these role descriptions something that everyone supports and can act on?

Next Step: Discuss co-operational points between the different roles. What expectations do the defensive players have on forwards etc. Visualize the outcome to all players.

Set goals for the team - Team building exercise

How: Discuss with the whole group what goal you should have for the whole season.

What sub-goals can you set up? (In October we have... Until Christmas we have...)

Can forwards / defenders / goalkeepers have their own goals? (We will not let in more goals than x / match / We will block x number of shots per game)

When you are done with the main and sub-goals, divide the players into groups.

They should now think about what they are going to do to achieve the goals. Define concrete activities.

To discuss:

Do the goals feel stimulating/engaging?

Are they worth fighting for?

Are all ready to put down the work you have described?

Part 2:

What soft goals can you set up? (E.g. How you should be and act as a team – Values, rules and norms)

How can you measure it? (E.g. A questionnaire with questions around each topic and how each player in the team on a scale 1-5, see we are progressing/Living the values)

Find the right team - Team building exercise

Aim: Divide the team into sub-groups with a fun teambuilding activity. Highlight the importance of communication out on the ice and also in the booth.

How: Find the correct team - Write several different hockey teams on paper slips. All the players take a note without showing it to anyone else. Ideally everyone should have a blindfold / hat for the eyes, but you can also turn off the light and ask the players to close their eyes. Then it's time to find their "teammates / players in the same club"

A more difficult variant can be to use known players' names from the different clubs and that the players thereby group themselves into the right team. Or writing first and second part of the team name on few slip e.g. Edmonton on one slip – Oilers on another.

To discuss:

How did you find each other? Easy? Difficult?

Was anyone having trouble finding their group? Why?

What made you find each other? (...communication)

How can it be out on hockey plan? Do we need to find each other there?

Are we talking enough to each other out on the ice? How did this exercise work if we hadn't talked to each other?

Can you give some concrete examples of when we need to talk to each other on ice (game situations)?

How is the communication in the booth, can we talk more there?

Did some good ideas pop up on how we can improve our communication during training or matches?

What was the purpose of the exercise? (The question can be asked to see what the players have learned.)

Combine the right player together - Team building exercise

Purpose: Divide into pairs with a fun teambuilding activity.

Highlight the importance of communication out on the ice and also in the booth.

How: Forming pairs (first name + surname, Mats + Sundin) write several different hockey players names on paper slips. First name on one and last name on another. All the players take note without showing it to anyone else. Ideally everyone should have a blindfold / hat for the eyes, but you can also turn off the light and ask the players to close their eyes. Then it is time to mate with help of the names, for example, Mats need to find Sundin, these two will form a pair (perhaps for the next exercise that you will do in pairs).

To discuss:

How did you find each other? Easy? Difficult?

Was anyone having trouble finding their pair? Why?

What made you find each other? (...communication)

How can it be out on hockey rink? Do we need to find each other there?

Are we talking enough to each other out on the ice? How did this exercise work if we hadn't talked to each other?

Can you give some concrete examples of when we need to talk to each other on ice (game situations)?

How is the communication in the booth, can we talk more there?

What was the purpose of the exercise? (The question can be asked to see what the players have learned.)

Dissolve "human knot" - Team building exercise

Purpose: To practice collaboration and communication.

How: Human knot - After dividing the players into sub-groups, ask them to form a circle in groups. When you say, everyone should close their eyes and go towards the middle and grab the hand of two different people. When everyone has grasped the hands of two different people, they can open their eyes. Now it is important to solve the knot without releasing your hands and forming a circle again.

To discuss:

How did you think it went? Easy? Difficult?

What made you succeed in solving the knot? (... Cooperation) If not everyone had helped each other, did you succeed?

Were you forced to talk a lot? How did it work? Did everyone talk at once, one who was talking or one at a time?

How should we talk to each other?

How good are we at helping each other out on the ice?

What can we improve on when it comes to collaboration on the ice?

What are we doing well today?

How can we help each other with the help of communication?

Was anyone angry? Why?

How did that affect the group?

How should we handle such situations?

What was the purpose of the exercise? (The question can be asked to see what the players have learned.)

Paintball light - Team building exercise

Purpose: To practice collaboration, strategy and communication. Can also be used for off season training to build on fitness.

How: Paintball "light" - You need to have a small forest area to be in.

Divide your group into two groups. One group is provided with water-soluble felt pens and an object, for example a flag / hockey stick to defend. The group with the pencils and the flag / hockey stick is sent to an area further away, where they are to place their flag / hockey stick visible and then hide in the "forest". The second team goes to their starting position and then tries to get to the flag / hockey stick. The defending team may make a marker with the pencil on the opponent's hand when they succeed in catching an "enemy". If you are caught you need to count to e.g. 50 before continuing.

To discuss:

How was the exercise?

What was the purpose?

Did you put up any tactics before?

How did you cooperate?

Could you have cooperated more?

Can you mention any element in which you cooperated?

Can you touch any moment that you had managed

better if you had cooperated?

Are there some similarities to how we act on the ice?

Can we bring something from this exercise that we have with us in the future?

Goal

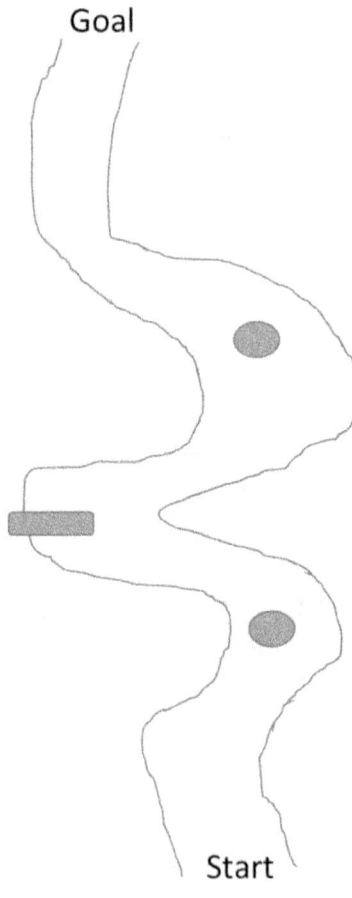

Start

Water rafting - Team building exercise

Purpose: To highlight the importance of communication, to trust each other and to talk one at a time.

How: Rafting - draw a river on A4 with some obstacles on the way. The group should not see the "map" until they have appointed one to "go" (draw with the pen). The one who will go on the river must listen to instructions from the others. If he / she goes off the water or on an obstacle it is over and you need to start from the beginning. Compete some groups against each other.

To discuss:

How did the exercise go? What was hard?

How was the communication? Did everyone talk at once, why?

When where you most successful / had most progress, how was the communication?

How should we communicate with each other? (One at a time etc.) What more is important to think about?

If these things are important, how does it look like today in our team?

How can we make sure that we communicate better with each other?

Did the one who was having the pencil, trust the information?

Do we also always trust each other's information, rumors / bullshit / talk behind someone's back?

How should we handle rumors / bullshit / talk behind someone's back?

What was the purpose of the exercise?

Remember - Team building exercise

Purpose: To practice co-operation. Ask if something is unclear.

How: Remember Things - Take a newspaper (sports section / hockey magazine) and put 5-10 things (whatever, pen, puck, tape roll ...) on it, ask the players to watch all things for 60 seconds. Then they sit in a group and discuss what things they remember, for five minutes. Then you ask what was in the headline of the newspaper.

To discuss:

If you hadn't asked about the headlines, how many things did the players remember?

Why didn't they count with the magazine? (If they didn't?)

Was anyone asking about the newspaper? Why not?

How is it when you are going to run an ice practice, then you ask if you do not understand?

How can we improve on it in the future?

How was the communication when you were in the group?

Was everyone "allowed" to speak?

Was there someone who "ran" over the others in the team work?

How should we be against each other in such situations, what is Important to remember?

What was the purpose of the exercise? (The question can be asked to see what the players have learned.)

Carry a hockey stick - Team building exercise

Purpose: Collaboration, helping each other and communicating.

How to: Carry a hockey stick - Divide the players into groups. All groups must have a hockey stick. The practice is that everyone should hold the stick without dropping it (not allowed to grip the stick, just carry with open hand palm) and getting around a track.

If someone lets go, the team must form a ring by holding each other in the hands around the stick before they pick it up again and can continue the exercise.

To discuss:

How was the exercise?

What was the purpose?

What worked well / worse?

How was the communication? Positive / Negative-whiny?

If negative why?

Does the negative communication help the group?

How is the communication within the team?

Is there any difference when it goes well, against when it goes worse, when you e.g. are behind during a match?

How should we try to talk to each other? (Positive, concrete, encouraging, instructing how to do it instead of talking about what error we have done...)

What was the purpose of the exercise? (The question can be asked that you should see what the players have learned.)

Reduce the number of card stacks - Team building exercise

Purpose: To learn to work together towards a common solution

How to: Divide the group into smaller groups of 3-5 people.

Give each group 16 cards, which they put on a table, 4 cards in each row and 4 rows.

The group will now reduce the number of cards / stacks to one or as few as possible.

The cards can be moved horizontally or vertically, not diagonally any distance.

The card being moved must always be placed on top of another card. The empty surfaces can't be used.

The cards can only be placed on top of another card of the same suit or rank. (e.g. hearts on hearts and 9 on 9...)

When a card is on top of another, they move like a pile. The underlying cards lose their value.

You are unable to undo a move.

The groups now have 10 minutes to complete.

Which group has the least number of card heights on the table.

To discuss:

How did you put up the strategy?

Did all of the solutions come up? Why not? Was there someone who "withdrew"? Why?

How can this be linked to training / match?

What is team spirit - Team building exercise

Purpose: To get players to discuss attitudes and to have the right attitude towards each other and also to opponents.

How: Discuss in Group:

What is team spirit?

How does a winning team act against each other within the team?

How / What is a winning attitude?

How can we create joy, what should we do to create it?

How to show respect?

To discuss further:

Discuss the things that come up in good team spirit more concrete.

E.g. If good team spirit is to be good friend, how are you a good friend, what do you do as a good friend?

Have fun, what are you doing to get things fun? Feeling as one team, how do you do it?

Positive communication during training - Team building exercise

Purpose: To develop the positive communication between the players and to strengthen their self-confidence.

How to: Give your players the task of giving at least one concrete positive comment to all other players during a training session. E.g. you had good speed. Nice fake. Nice shot. Thanks for the nice pass.

After the training, everyone should write down the comments they remember, which they have received during the training. Save the notes collectively or individually.

To discuss:

How did it feel to get so many positive comments?

How many comments did the players remember?

Was it easier to remember some? Why?

How did it feel to give feedback to the others?

Was it easy / difficult? Why?

What do you think this will bring?

Team rules - Team building exercise

Purpose: To create common rules for training and match.

Method: Divide the players into groups and let them discuss the following:

How should it look before training, when we arrive? Warm up? Review of the training before? How should the locker room look after the end of training...

As for the game, take the help of previous questions.

What about bus trips?

What applies to away games?

If you violate the rules, what consequences should this have?

To discuss:

Ask all groups to explain what they have come up with.

Agree in common what rules you should choose and follow.

Compile the rules and ask all players to sign.

Hang up in the storage room / changing room / hand out to all.

Create goal image - Team building exercise

Purpose: To create a positive target image and to strengthen self-confidence and team spirit.

How: Divide the players into groups, ask them to create a newspaper's front page about what you have achieved together after the season.

Put up the posters in the storage room / changing room / hand out to all to be set up at home.

Teamwork Collaboration losses

Leadership responsibility		Team Responsibility			
		Teamwork			
Energy / Engagement	Direction / Goals	Capacity	+ Team Spirit	− Collaboration losses	Results (Hard and soft)
Feedback and learning					

The last part of the teamwork block is about collaboration losses. This is the part you should try to reduce, in order to improve your team's performance and results, using tools and methods such as feedback, training, drills, team building and other activities that improve teamwork.

Collaboration losses can be described as the opposite of team spirit, but also as more practical losses during a practice or match referring back to capacity:

Lack of...

- How to use the training time (quality in training)
- Communication
- Equipment
- Skills
- Experience
- Satisfaction
- Support around the team (ass. Coachers, goalkeeper coach)
- Common goals
- Honesty
- Loyalty
- Positive
- Commitment
- Problem solving
- Communication
- Supporting each other
- Ethics
- Moral
- Norms and values

Collaboration losses can also be:

- Undefined roles
- Bad passes
- Not synchronized activities
- Poor timing
- Wrong or incorrect positioning
- Poor performance
- Errors during the exercises on your training
- Unclear directive
- We and them thinking or me and you (in a negative way)
- Selfish behavior (in a negative way)

Ringelmann study – "Tug of war" / Pull the rope

One of the earliest studies in collaboration losses and social loafing was made by Ringelmann.

Ringelmann let people participate in a "tug of war" experiment. He began by measuring everyone's individual capacity (strength), which was defined as 100%. Then they did the "tug of war" exercise in pairs, with three people, four people and so on. The results showed that in pairs, the people reached 93% of their capacity, when they were three people in the team in the tug of war, they reached 85% of their individual capacity, 77% in a team of four and only 49% in a team of eight people, (capacity + team spirit) - cooperation losses = performance. So in a group of 8 people you only got 49% of the individual capacity due to collaborative losses and possibly a little "socially loafing".

The tendency for people's efforts to decrease in a larger group is sometimes called the "Ringelmann effect", his studies are also supported by later studies (Ingham, Levinger, Graves & Peckham, 1974).

This may explain why some star players are sometimes invisible during a match, waiting for the other players to work and not counting that their own low performance will be visible.

Often it can be the opposite, many of the team members take a step back and wait for the star player to win the match for the team. This type of social loafing will be displayed at all levels, at all ages and regardless of gender.

With these conditions, there are two parts that you should try to improve, your capacity and team spirit and reduce cooperation losses, as much as possible.

Social loafing as a result of a penalty?

Many times at younger ages it becomes visible in a power play that the team that should have an advantage, does not actually have it and some find it strange that you cannot cope with the advantage from a power play.

Firstly, we are talking about younger players, then it is not obvious that the game works in all situations, it can be a cause.

The other aspect is linked to social loafing, we have an advantage, I do not have to do the job as hard as usual, we are after all a man more, while the team in the box play position thinks the opposite and the effect is as described and sometimes very clearly in the younger teams.

Here you as a coach can play an important role, keeping the players focused and pushing them to play as focused and with same speed as before.

Social loafing can also be visible after a red card in football, the team with the advantage of having a player more than the opposite team sometimes tends to step back and feel comfortable (social loafing), instead of continuing as they did before. The team of only ten players can feel that they need to take greater responsibility and therefore the game can continue to look like they are playing with even strength.

Smooth collaboration to minimize collaborative losses

Make the different parts of your team work together smoothly, the team composition is important to avoid collaborative losses.

Training with the same speed and intensity as in the game is obvious to every coach, otherwise you will face "new" a situation during a match because you have practiced your skills at a lower speed.

In order to avoid social loafing and the collaborative losses associated with it, you need to have clear roles, responsibilities and standards in your team.

(Social loafing - I don't have to do my best, no one will see it)

"Elite initiative", "Level adaption", "Shortening the bench"...

Three words or combination of words, Elite initiative, Level adaptation and shortening the bench, are words that can also be linked to collaborative losses and social loafing.

If we start with my definitions of these words, then:

Elite initiative is a hard training team (not age-dependent), where you pick up the best players for the moment and changes can be made during and before the coming season. Other sports are usually not "allowed".

Shortening the bench can be close at hand for an elite team, it is about winning and then playing the best when required, e.g. at the end of the matches. Benching, can of course, occur and also occurs in teams that do not have a pronounced elite initiative.

The level adjustment for me is that everyone is involved, but that during the training the players are matched according to the model "birds of a feather stick together", you practice with players on the same level (minimize cooperation losses). It gives the greatest challenges to all players, the best meet the best and develop, (here I was going to start writing avoidance), but I write in plain text, the worse meet worse and then someone(s) in that group get to be the best in that group during the training and everyone gets the chance to succeed and the opportunity to build on their own capacity, by exercising at the level where they are at the moment, this will change during the year and coming years, depending on how much force is put into building up the capacity (train) in each individual.

 Therefore, it is also important for me to constantly analyze and test the levels of different players, so there are no static groups. The same principle applies to the matches, all players playing games, but preferably against a teams that is closest to match their current maturity or competence level. Rather a 3-2 win or loss, than 10-1 in any direction.

I advocate level adjustment and can understand the elite initiative in some clubs, but not as widely as it is right now...

Is it possible to train with a few pucks?

Is it possible to carry out a training with e.g. four pucks (four stations), or will it create time and collaboration losses?

It is clear that it is feasible if you play every exercise until finish, goalkeeper or player / players who have just finished the first part of the hockey drill, continue to play back, or transport the puck at high speed to the starting position, so that none of the hockey drills ends with just one shot to the goal, and then returning back to the queue, then the next shot...

Below an example of a hockey drill, where one puck is enough.

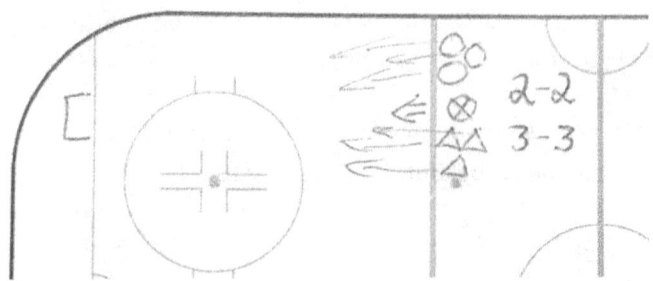

The coach / player shoots at goal. 2 against 2 or 3 against 3 (two attackers, two defenders), when the defenders manage to win the puck, they pass the puck back to the coach / leader and become forwards (quick role change), seek position, get a pass and attack when they have finished playing , the puck in goal, blocked or back in the lead. Start a new sequence with shot against goal.

In the capacity section, we have touched on different types of passes, i.e. different types of skills when it comes to pass, but the execution always takes place in interaction with someone else and a poor performance creates collaborative losses, the better and more accurate the players are with the passes and reception, the lower the collaborative losses will be and we have the opportunity to achieve higher and better results.

For some passing drills, please return back to the capacity section and pick the passing drills there.

Teamwork Collaboration losses
- Passing

Deliver a good pass

When delivering a pass, you should think of the following steps, the puck ready on the blade, eye contact or communication with the pass recipient, the body weight from the back to the front foot, sweeping away the puck and acting immediately after the pass (move to a new position), the game continues even after a good pass.

Receive a pass

When receiving a pass, you should consider the following steps, the stick on the ice, communicate, show where you want the puck, see the surroundings (what do you do in the next step), take in the puck softly (follow with the blade in the puck direction).

Reception of a deep-pass

When receiving a deep-pass, which comes directly from behind, the angle of the blade perpendicular to the direction pass comes from, in order to be able to catch the puck.

If the blade is not angled correctly, you will not be able to control the puck quickly.

Look up the sequence before, so that the player is aware of the surroundings and immediately after receiving.

A simple exercise on receiving deep passes is of course going in pairs one after the other moving forward, a little closer at the beginning and with longer distances to increase the difficulty level.

Reception of pass with skate

In addition to receiving a pass on the blade, you can of course receive a pass in other ways too, the skate, with the hand or with the other body.

When receiving on the skate, the purpose is to get the puck to the stick blade as quickly as possible. It can be done by tilting the skate and steering the puck at the right angle, or stopping the puck and getting it through a light kicking movement or stopping the puck and taking it with the stick where it is located. Look up before and immediately after reception.

Pass reception with glove and body

Pucks that come rushing above the ice are always the easiest and safest to try to get down to the blade with the glove. Look up before and immediately after reception.

Sometimes you can't get your hand out, then you have to stop the puck with the other parts of the body, try to get as large and collected body surface as possible behind the puck at the moment of reception.

A simple exercise can consist of that in pairs "flip" high pucks to each other, this step can also be built in at the beginning of a drill, start the drill by picking up a high pass (it can be someone who just throws a puck to be picked down).

Practice odd pass receptions

Just as with regular passes, you need to practice on the odd variants, train on receiving the pass on the skate, glove and with the body.

Here, for example a trainer throws pucks in the beginning to really get the exercise right.

One more drill containing an odd pass reception as a sub-element in the drill.

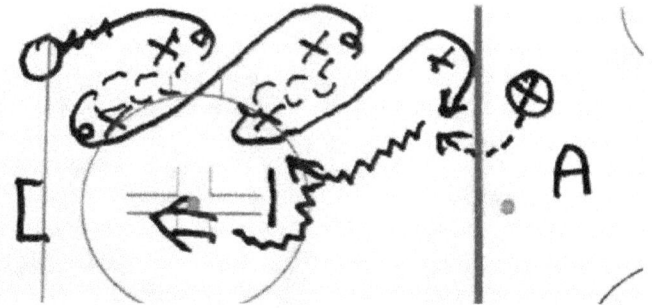

Hockey drill A: Forward and backwards around the cones with or without puck. At blue, a leader or other player throws a puck in the air, which the player takes down with his hand, makes a fake and finishes. If the exercise is started with the puck, it is passed to the player who throws the puck and then stops the pass with his feet's, while the player throws the puck to the buddy.

Teamwork Collaboration losses
- Face offs

Face offs

During a face off, it is important to have a plan for where the puck should end up, and a clear division of roles, who does what.

The one taking the face off is always in charge of the situation and controls the setup, roles and actions that have been made in advance.

In and immediately after the actual face off situation, all the players must be on the toe and act directly the puck is released, if it is about direct shot, block players or make themselves playable, then everyone must act quickly and synchronized (to minimize or create collaborative losses).

Face offs require practice, just as any other skill or game situation.

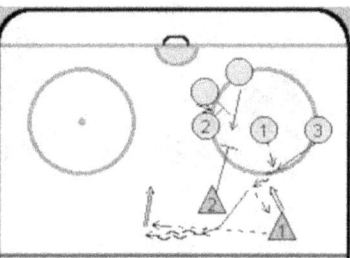

Teamwork Collaboration losses
- Game understanding

A technical robot or a creative "artist"

A technical hockey robot that follows instructions or a creative hockey artist? For me personally, the choice is simple, I prefer the creative players who understand the game and can make their own decisions in difficult situations, although technical robots may also be required in today's ice hockey.

 With today's little distorted focus being the best already at the age of 10 and the technical skill of today's children, training and development are driving more towards "robotization" of the great mass according to me.

The truth is that the most attractive players for the audience are not the robots but the creative artists who take the hockey to the next level. One does not exclude the other, everyone cannot be artists, but you may be a robot with your own brain?

Creative or board out and dump puck?

I think the answer is simple and that you should teach the players to try to be creative and dare to keep the puck, and find the pass rather than e.g. put it out by the board, it does not mean that this should go to the extreme, that it is ugly or forbidden to shoot out or dump the puck into the offensive zone. It's about finding a balance, first creative, get rid of pressure (using skating and stick handling skills), create time, pass and as a last option, board out or dump the puck.

If you play board out in a smart way passing the puck on a free surface where a teammate can catch it is an excellent and a creative solution, the same applies at the entrance in the attack zone, use the board to play the puck inside the blue past a defenseman on a free surface.

Understanding the game

In order to be able to use the game understanding out on the ice, the basic skills needs to be in place and then especially skating, without skating no play.

The understanding of the game as a technical element is interesting because you cannot see it outside of a player, the player can be strong, fast and have a good shot in individual steps on the hockey exercises, but the game understanding becomes visible only when everything is connected in match situations in interlinked skills.

There you can get both positive and negative surprises, but as long as skating is there, there is no worries. Game understanding can be practiced through games, coaching and theory.

The understanding of the game is mainly about understanding your own and the opponents' game and acting on it in a right way. To take decisions and act in the situation that has arisen and to evaluate and learn from what works and what does not.

Game understanding through spontaneous hockey and public skating

Today, the game range and the technical equipment for playing games on different consoles, mobiles and tablets are available in all homes. Does this also mean that spontaneous sports are gone, which builds up game understanding (capacity) and thereby also minimizes cooperation losses?

Are there still some players who actually plays street hockey, create their own leagues or shoot penalties on the street? I believe that, this very basic training and training of game understanding has almost died.

The lack of spontaneous games obviously affects the hockey coach, the spontaneous game needs to move in to the training or to its connection, to teach our hockey players to be creative, find their own solutions and create a learning around the game. Could it be a pre-practice activity, play street hockey as warm up?

There you will get some important lessons:
That works, that didn't work, although I try it again...

How to practice game understanding?

If we start by looking at concepts that are usually inserted into game understanding, the following areas occur:

- Game perception and or pattern recognition
- Game intelligence
- Problem solving
- Split Vision
- Automation

- Roll Acceptance
- Cognitive ability

Problem solving is a key for me, it means that you do not have too controlled game drills, 2 against 2 or 3 against 3 on a limited area with different starting positions on the track and different ways to start the exercise.

3 on 2 – 3 mot 2 – 3 vastaan 2

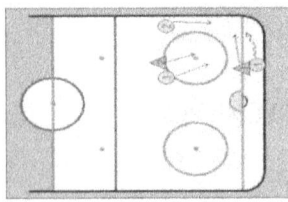

P1 starts with puck. P2 into the corner to create a 2-1 situation against D1. 3-2 until the puck is dead (goal, the goalkeeper has it or out from the zone).

P1 startar med puck. P2 ut i hörnet, för att skapa en 2-1 situation mot D1. 3-2 tills pucken är död (mål, målvakten har den eller den har spelats ut ur zon).

P1 aloittaa kiekon kanssa. P2 nurkkaan tekemään 2-1 tilanteen D1 vastaan. 3-2 kunnes kiekko on kuollut (maalissa, maalivahdilla tai pois alueelta).

This will strengthen many of the other areas. The exercises can also be started with a battle that can be automated, e.g. 1 vs 1 at the board with a puck and then the drill moves over to 2 vs 2 or 3 vs 3.

You get good at what you practice on is maybe a little overused and therefore a boring statement to hear, but still true, the more times you are exposed to different situations and problems the better you get to solve these.

Game understanding via mobile and tablet

As I have mentioned earlier, most children and young people today have a mobile and probably also a tablet/computer, which they spend a lot of time using.

How can this be turned into something positive that benefits the perception of the game? The latest research says that you can train the game understanding visually. Watching game moments from YouTube or NHL.com strengthens the game understanding.

How can you get your players to watch hockey on YouTube? One way may be that the players are given the task, to find the best pass or goal (which is not a shootout or penalty shot) and share this with their friends, via social media, before training, or describe how it was made, to get the others want to see the clip online. Make game situations on YouTube a topic of conversation, before each practice.

Game with puck in attack zone

Hockey games require creativity, movement and practice. Here it is about building something, which is always more difficult than destroying or tearing down.

Creativity is primarily about individual skill to find solutions to retain the puck within the team, but at least as important are the non-puck driver's movement and creativity, that they make themselves playable, tempo changes and place changes are two effective tools, and that everyone wants and is ready to get the puck.

A simple exercise that includes Creativity, individual skill to find solutions to keep the puck within the team, movement, playability, pace and place changes, on a small surface.

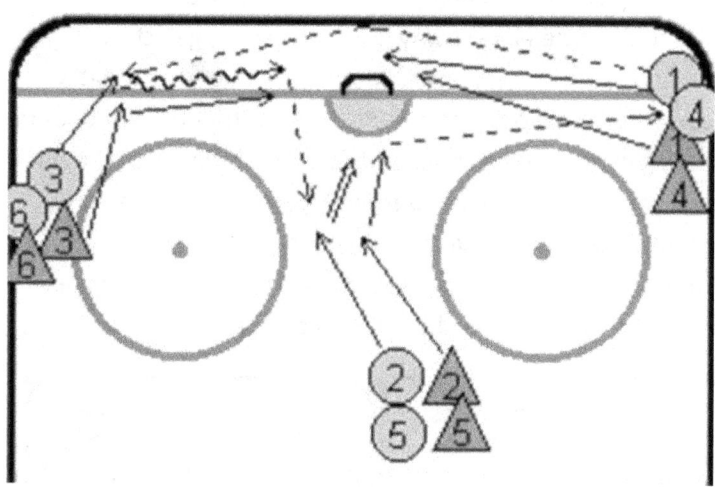

Break out under pressure and steering

When the opponents put pressure directly after a puck loss, all players without puck must act quickly and assist the pressed puck driver. The puck driver must always have a pass-option to the side, backward and forward, with max 3 passes you must be in the middle zone.

When the opponents set up for steering, it is about "getting rid of" the opponents first position or the player closest to puck holder. The easiest way is to create a 2 against 1 situation against that player, i.e. that the puck driver has at least two passing options, this also means that the opponents steering player has to choose whether he is there for the puck holder or the first or second free player. If he goes for the first, pass to number two or if the steering player goes for number two, then the pass goes to number one or the puck driver himself can drive the puck up on the ice.

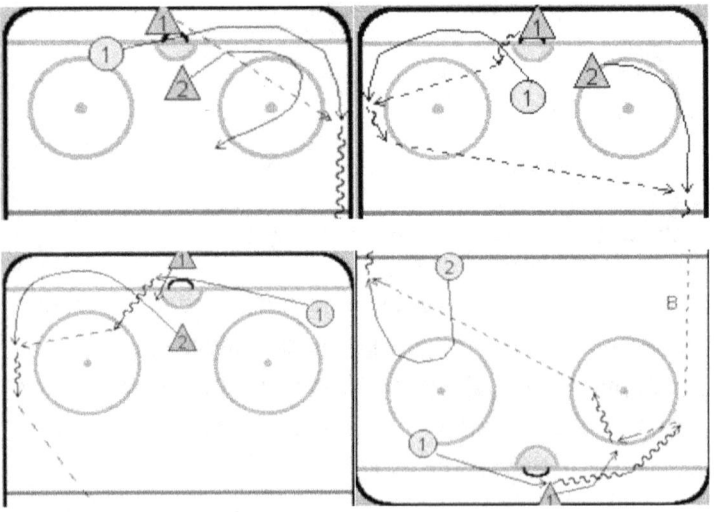

The steering practice as such can also be used as a skating drill at the beginning of a practice (practicing to create collaborative losses for the opponents)

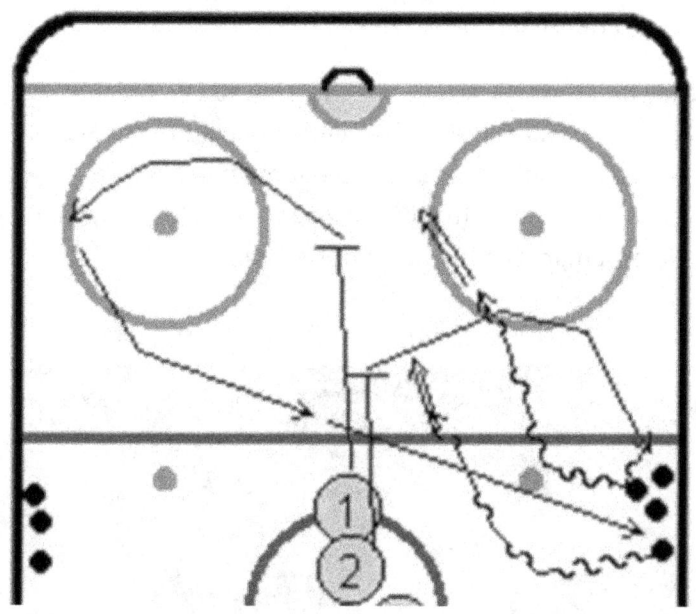

Players 1 and 2 take the position to steer, (imagined player in behind goal, who drops and plays on the other side) player 1 steering deep, goes back to the middle, player 2 steers towards the other board higher up the ice, player 2 takes puck and goes straight to the finish, player 1 also picks up puck and then finishes (player 2 screens / steers in front of goal and takes any rebounds).

In games, there are of course many simple variations to practice, you will find a lot on HockeyCoach.se in the eBook Offensive plays and break outs (just drawings, no text explanations).

Entering offensive zone via 2 vs. 1

Getting into the attack zone with high speed and trying to get down deep towards the goal is number one, but usually there are obstacles on the blue line in the form of a defender, easiest here as well is to create a 2 against 1 situation against the defenseman. See below for one example.

2 on 1 – 2 mot 1 – 2 vastaan 1

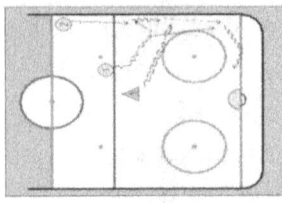

P1 skates in with the puck. D1 follows. P1 drops the puck to P2 and skates towards the short end. P2 pass the puck to P1 along the border. 2-1 towards the goal.

P1 in i zon med puck. D1 följer med. P1 droppar till P2 och åker mot kortändan. P2 passar pucken djupt längs med sargen. 2-1 mot mål.

P1 luistelee kiekon kanssa, D1 seuraa. P1 syöttää P2 ja luistelee päätyä kohti. P2 syöttää kiekon laitaa pitkin päätyyn. 2-1 maalia kohti.

After the entrance, the puck driver targets the goal, either by skating towards the goal, or seeking a pass, or taking a shot. The player who came in to the zone immediately after the puck driver must always go at the highest speed towards the goal, the possible third attacker looking for the far back surface. The puck inside blue and ready for pass and direct shot.

At all shots, it is a matter of having players in front of the goalkeeper to screen, steer and take rebounds. If there is a rebounds, it is important to win the fight against the defensive player and really give everything and show the will to get to the puck, these are situations you should try to include in your practices, 1 vs 1 battle towards goal and a rebound.

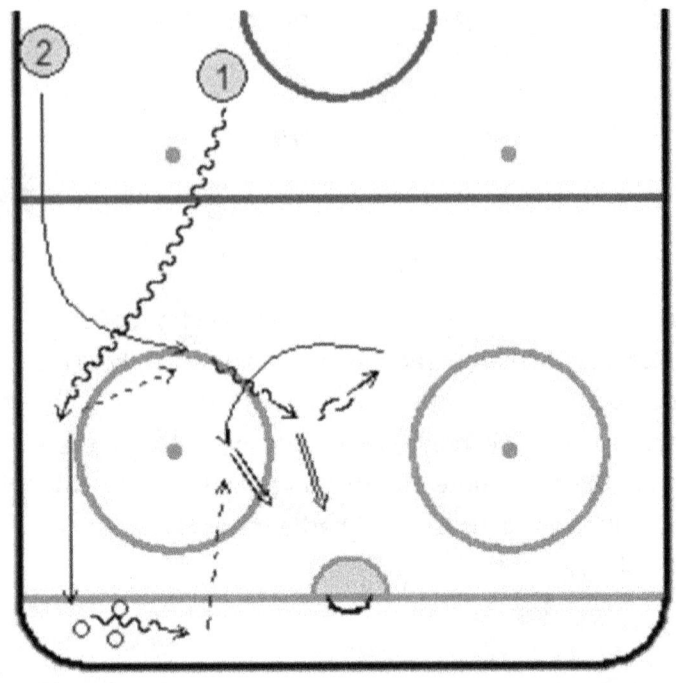

A two against zero exercise that you easily change to a 2 against 1 after a while.

Turnovers in the middle zone

A dropped puck out of the offensive zone is an opportunity for a quick turnover, if you see it in a positive way.

Some guidelines are that the first player out of the zone goes on the far side of the puck holder, the other goes on the puck side. The third takes the surface in the middle.

The puck driver should quickly have three passing options forward, one sideways and one backwards. A side or backward pass is ok, but then the game has to move forward, in order to be able to take advantage of the quick turnover.

The one who gets the pass will of course take the puck quickly towards the goal again, the second at the highest speed against the goal, the third on the far rebound surface, the defensive players on blue.

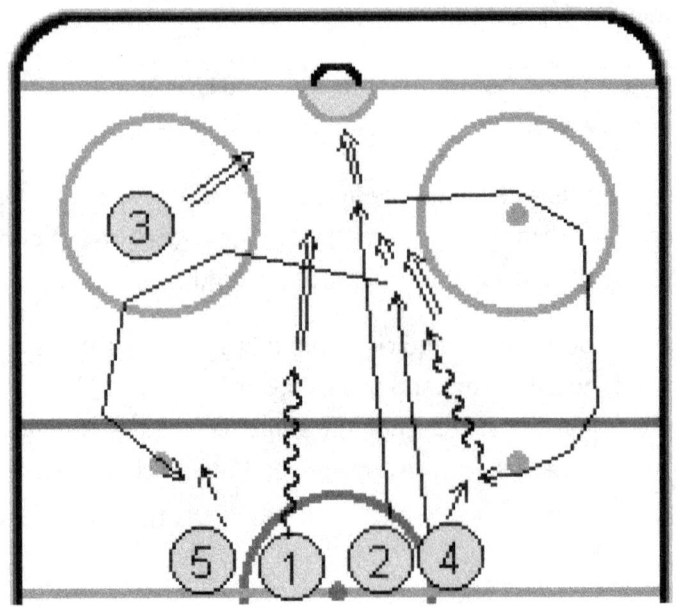

An exercise on the theme, with entrance in the middle of zone in this example.

Player 1 enters and finishes, player 2 goes for the rebound, player 2 turns up towards blue after the rebound, meanwhile player 3 shoots a close shot, when player 2 has come over blue, he gets pass from player 4 who goes after player 2 who finishes, player 4 goes for the rebound, then turns up towards blue... The example is with entrance in the middle, but you can of course have the entrance on one of the sides, rebound taker goes then in from middle with full speed towards the goal.

Hockey is 1 against 1?

We continue a little bit with training and practice principles. During a hockey game you have 5 against 5, but if you look closer you can apply the rule from the mathematics "Lowest common denominator", in which case you will always have 1 against 1 situations in the hockey rink.

If you can fool a player or support a fellow player better than the other team, you will have a 2 against 1 situation and therefore an advantage! Why should we actually try to complicate drills and practices with, for example, running a drill with more than 3x (1 against 1), 3 against 3?

"The way I use to develop an aerobic state is three against three, one against one, in a square of 20 meters by 20 meters." / José Mourinho

"Everything must be kept simple, don't complicate what is a simple thing, a simple beautiful game" / Luiz Felipe Scolari

Hockey 50% 1 against 1, and 35% 2 against 2

85% of the hockey games consist of 1 against 1 or 2 against 2 situations, 50% 1 against 1, and 35% 2 against 2. Therefore, the emphasis in game drills on the practices also needs to be in 1 against 1 and 2 against 2 situations, since this is the most common game situations a player is exposed to the most.

 A small area 1 against 1 or 2 against 2, in varying places on the ice is the best training, which I have been in and touched earlier

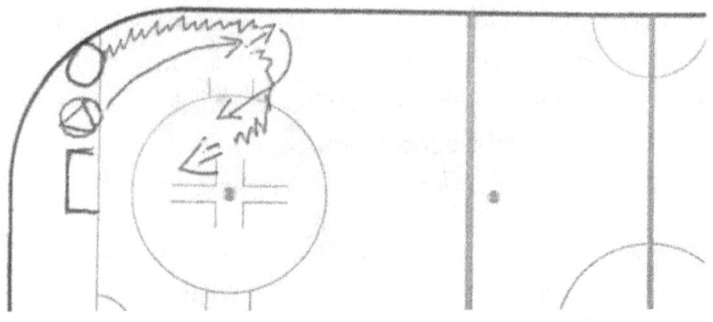

Example of a 1 against 1 exercise.

One player with puck starts next to the board, the other attacks by lifting the stick or using body contact. Both try to score, play until the puck is in goal or blocked.

Practicing on a narrow and limited surface develops the understanding of the game, skills and it makes the exercise match like, the more often you train on this type of situation on a training, the greater the probability of success during a match.

Some more 1 vs 1 drills for you to use:

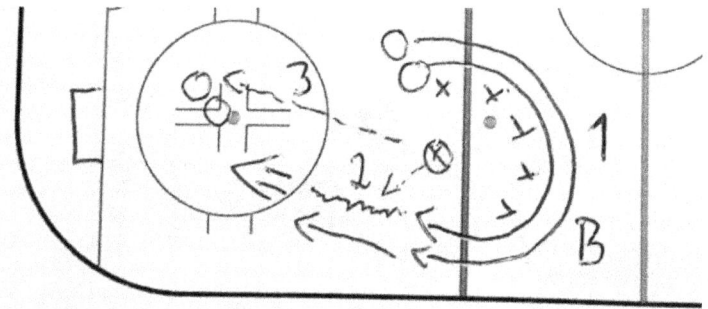

Hockey drill B 1. Players start simultaneously 2. Pass from the coach, battle against goals, when the situation is over 3. New puck against goal, one against one in front of goal, search for a quick finish.

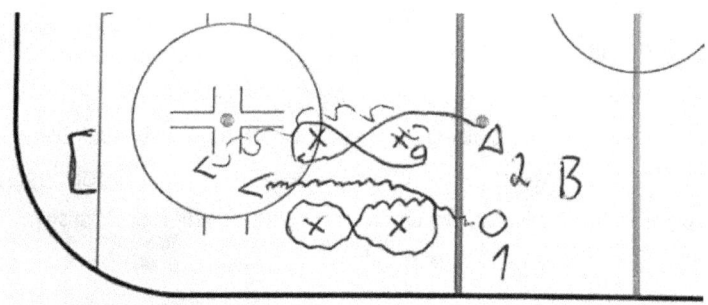

Hockey drill B 1. The striker starts with a puck, skating in an eight around the cones 2. The defender goes first forward around the cones in an eight, and the last bit backwards. Play the 1 vs 1 situation to the end.

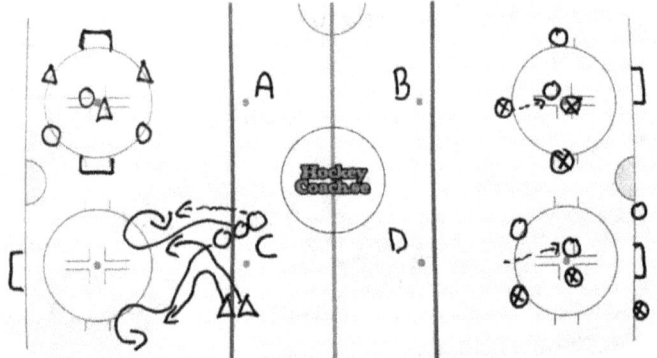

Hockey drill A: 1 against 1 in the circle with two shooters on both sides.

Hockey drill B: 1 against 1 in the circle with a shooter to each player.

Hockey drill C: 2 vs. 2, one pair starts attacking, the other defending. Enter the zone and make you playable, pass from the attackers from your own lead. 2 against 2 until puck in goal, blocked, or played back to the lead, then the defenders become attackers and forwards defenders, quick conversion, pass from the lead to those who attack.

Hockey drill D: 1 against 1 in the circle with a shooter and a passer to both players.

Game understanding through small area games

Small team play 2 against 2, 3 against 3 or 4 against 4 is perhaps the optimal exercise for game understanding. Here the players are exposed to lots of quick decisions, adjustments, puck contact and all the time with <u>limited time and space</u>. An additional aspect to focus on in the small team game is to bring the communication, "I'm in the middle", "behind", "watch out", "you have time", "shoot" etc.

 Small team games provide the opportunity to repeat lots of moments in a good match like environment and create pattern recognition in "real" matches and it's also a great opportunity for you as a coach to work with feedback to your players.

In the small games you can also include some specific skills that you have practiced on the drills before. E.g. you have been practicing "mohawks", you could therefore say that before a pass is allowed in the small area game you need to do a "Mohawk". With this your players immediately learn how and where to apply a "new skill" in a game situation.

Summary of guidelines on game understanding

Good skating together with good body control are A and O, both in attack and defense.

Attack - Playable, away from "passing shadow". Create width and depth. Win the inside against the goal. Create triangles or boxes around the puck driver. Find solutions, be creative and act quickly.

Defense - Play on the right side, between goal and striker. Turn your head, where are the attackers, where can the pass come? Reduce the time and shrink the surfaces for the attackers. Act quickly at puck gain, quick turnover or switch from defense to attack.

Passing

Passing is the part of the game that does not get better because you struggle and struggle, but it is about coordination and fine motoric eye and hand cooperation, as well as focusing on the actual pass, but also in the reception.

It doesn't matter how fast a player is on the skates, the puck always goes faster. However, a good skate technique and balance are required, in order to get a good pass, especially in motion.

Good pass and skating raises the pace of the game, there is probably nothing that is more difficult than "chasing puck".

Pass technique is also something that can be practiced outside of the ice using a green biscuit or wooden ball on asphalt/concrete or on a slightly longer shot plate or synthetic ice.

To challenge or to be challenged

Many times, hockey coaches talk about challenging another player or a defender in a game situation, but what does it really mean and what pictures do our players have about this when we say so, challenge someone?

For me, "to challenge" means that a player with the puck needs to move to a free space and make the defensive player also move there to take on the challenge, if he / she does not, you are the winner. If the player goes straight towards the defenseman "to challenge" on his / her area, you are actually the one who will be challenged, and that is not what we want, but this is the way it is perceived most of the times when we say challenge, the players think in 99 cases of 100, that they should go to the defenseman and dribble past.

Game strategy and philosophy open or controlled?

The optimum is if there is a red thread in the whole club (between teams) around game strategy and philosophy, then it will also be easier with the movement of players between the age groups and when changing coaches, the players recognize themselves and can quickly be involved and productive in the game.

In other words, a completely open idea of the game does not work, and a completely controlled one neither for that part, unless you have the purpose of killing all creativity and joy.

However, there should be frames, guidelines and roles that the players can absorb and reconcile with, then you also assume responsibility for the action in the game.

The four roles of the game

Whatever game system or strategy you use, the action during the game can be divided into four roles, puck driver (attack), non-puck driver (attack), puck attacker (defense) and non puck attacker (defense).

It's between these roles your players should be able to switch quickly, i.e. switch between two different offensive roles (with or without puck) and two defense roles (closest to puck or away from the puck driver), as well as the game mode as such, offensive or defensive game.

How quickly you change or predict game situations shows the understanding of the game. Hockey exercises for game understanding can be built with a view to switch quickly between these roles. (An example of such an exercise is found earlier in this chapter)

In addition to the actual defense or attack role, a brief description of the role is included for these.

The attack role should strive to score goals, create time and space, while the defense role should take back the puck before it is in goal and reduce the time and shrink areas for the attackers, quite obviously when reading it, but is it that obvious to your players or all of your players?

Teamwork Collaboration losses
- Defensive playing

Defensive playing

In the defense game, the importance of physics automatically comes in as an important area. Therefore, we should look at some common defensive situations and the actions in them.

The defense player's task is to primarily win the puck, in the second place to disturb and delay. The physical defensive game is also about mutual respect, preferably hard, but never unjust.

Physical part of the game, skills and respect

In the physical game, the physical skills are weighed in and it is primarily about functional strength, being able to master and use the physics at high speed while maintaining balance in a tight situation.

The physical game is also largely about technical skills, getting right into the situation and winning puck.

Last but not least, it's all about respect, with good physics and the right skills, you don't have to play unjustly. Hockey is a sport with a lot of physical elements, where respect for the opponent should always be included in close-up situations.

Defensive plays - disturb and delay

If the attacker has a slight advantage (the defense is after), the defender should try to get a quick and low poke to the

attacks stick to disrupt, or cause the attacker to lose the puck control.

Here it is not in the first position about winning the puck directly, but more about disturbing and delaying the

attack and the puck driver, hopefully to win the puck in the next position.

Defensive plays - lift the stick

When the puck driver is at the side or in front, the technique of lifting the stick can be used to win back the puck. The action should be quick, distinct and timed (preferably in the outer

position of the striker).

The lower arm lifts the stick while the upper arm presses down at the knob. After that, the stick must quickly go down and the puck be moved aside in a different direction from the opponent.

Defensive plays - lock the stick

Another way than to hit the stick, or to lift the stick is to lock the stick for the opponent on the ice.

To be able to lock the opponent's stick, it must come quickly and surprisingly with the own stick over the attackers and put a heavy pressure on the ice. In the next position, it is about poking the puck towards a harmless area or to a fellow player.

Defensive plays – poke with the stick

When the puck driver will skate forward towards a defender who goes backwards, it is about poking the stick, or blade to stop the attack. You should always aim to have blade against blade (work with the right positioning of the blade depending on how the offensive player moves the puck).

The defensive player should always try to be in a position that the forward must choose the side of the board. The stick hand is retracted, the gaze on the player (chest) and a quick surprising shock with the stick forward, do not wobble without bumping into the stick and puck. After having encountered the stick, seek body contact with the striker to stop the move and continued play from the attacker.

Defensive plays – tackle continue with speed

In the situations where the defense decides to stop an attack with a body hit, you can do this and still maintain your own speed.

When the puck driver comes close to the board, the defense player pushes his hockey stick and arms over the puck driver's stick and arms and then pushes in his own body in front, with the stick hard against the ice and turning out of the situation while maintaining speed.

Defensive plays – tackle with stop for opponent

When the puck driver comes close to the board and intends to make a change of direction, the player can be stopped, the tacking player has one leg behind the player and moves the upper body (shoulder) in front of him and presses it against the board. The stick in the ice and pick the puck.

Defensive plays – 2 against 1 advantage

When a lone puck driver meets two defenders, the first one can step in to stop the puck driver and the other takes the puck.

When the puck driver comes close to the board, the nearest defender (tackling the player) puts one leg behind the player and moves the upper body (shoulder) in front of him and pushes it against the board, with the stick on the ice, which locks the puck driver's stick. The other defender picks up the puck.

Example of a 2 vs. 1 exercise or switch to 1 vs 2

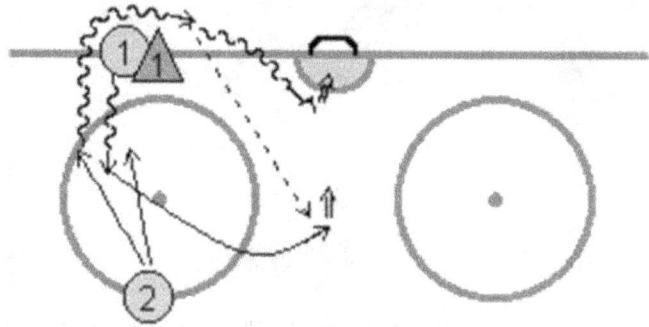

Defensive game - Blocking shots

Blocking shots is now more or less obvious area within the defense game, which is getting more and more focus. Using the statistics, ten covered shots during a hockey match correspond to 1 to 2 less allowed goals!

If you angle it in the way that, ten blocked shots from both forwards and defensive players will give you one to two less allowed goals per match, could perhaps increase the motivation to stand in front of the shooter instead of, to take the step aside, lift one leg up or not to go forward?

Blocking shots is all about courage

Standing in front of a shooter who gets off a shot requires primarily courage, but also the right technique.

The closer a player is to the shooter, the less "evil" it will do. At the same time, you increase the stress on the shooter and the chance to prevent that the shot comes at all.

The players today have good protection and it is important to rely on their equipment, shin guards, gloves, pants, shoulder protection and the helmet.

Here I have learned that you as coach sometimes need to check both the size and quality on the players equipment, all parents will not do that.

One way to practice blocking shots is, for example, that players shoot with tennis balls against blocking players.

When you get up the skills, the feeling will be "cool" when you block a shot, though it can sometimes hurt...

Here, the coaches with their feedback can strengthen the feeling of an important work, you saved a goal, with your block!

Teamwork Collaboration losses
- Box play

Box play / Penalty killing

Keep the opponents outside the area in front of the goalkeeper ("box out"), forwards playing defense remove the pass option.

Some guidelines for a successful box play.

- Always in the shooting line (between your own goal and the shooter, actually you should be between the puck and goal).

- Active movement with skates and hockey stick in the box to remove the plays through the box.

- Tough action in front of goal and on the rebound surfaces.

- Aggressive and moving players across the ice (in a smart way)

9 out of 10 goals are made from the surface in front of the goal, so make sure you are in that area ready to defend it.

On 10 power plays, 2-4 goals are made. Stay on the ice.

Turnovers - Game with puck

The majority of turnovers take place from the middle zone or the surface around the own blue line. Dropped pucks in these areas are due to poor mobility (playability / decision) in the attack game, dribbling instead of passing or placing the puck in the free surface in the attack zone.

Therefore, it is important with mobility and playability in the middle zone, pass with speed over the blue line. The puck driver (player 1) always tries to take the puck against goal via shot or pass (player 2). Players 2 always go against goals for pass or rebound. Player 3 comes in second wave for pass or for rebound in the far rebound area.

1-2 shots of 10 go in, that means, if you shoot between 10-15 shots, then you should probably keep your own goal clear to be able to win a match. If you manage to shoot 30 shots during a game, it could correspond to 6 goals scored.

Defensive game summary

No. 1, win the battle all over the ice, but above all in front of your own goal. Keep away opponents who come or are heading into the surface in front of goals.

- Dare to be creative in stressful situations, if you turn the game quickly in these situations, you create an advantage for attack. When shooting get the shot through and on target. One way to measure the success of the defense game can be to measure
- Number of stopped attacks in the middle zone
- Number of blocked shots
- Number of hits
- Number of won face offs

9 out of 10 goals are made from the surface in front of the goal, so make sure you are in that area as a defensive player.

Results

Leadership responsibility		Teamwork			Team Responsibility
Energy / Engagement	Direction / Goals	Capacity	+ Team Spirit	- Collaboration losesses	Results (Hard and soft)
Feedback and learning					

Results

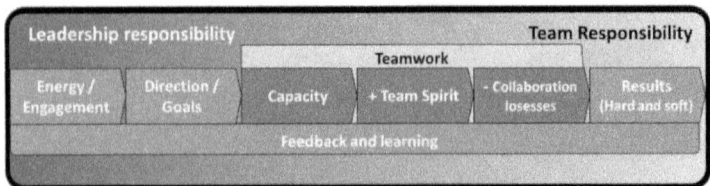

Results

What have we achieved? What results can you see? It is important to see both hard (objective) results, such as points, improved speed (time), skills (skill track on time) etc. But also to see the soft results, such as improved cooperation / teamwork, team spirit, communication, fighting spirit etc. The follow-up of the results is usually a minor problem in sport, than in many workplaces, for example.

In sports you have the points in the match, your league position, how many goals you have done, how many goals you have allowed, power play statistics etc. but in the workplace it can be more diffuse many times, how do you know you are doing a good job, or how do you know you are performing at work? Many companies strive for "world class", but have not defined it, or have no idea what it really means, or how their competitors perform, there is no league table available.

Visualize what you have achieved, hard and soft results. Small and large. Short and long term.

"We're not entertaining? Okay, I don't care, we win ..." / José Mourinho

If you have done your work in the direction block, with clarity in goals, focused areas, followed up on it and visualized it, this result block becomes much easier. You can see your results because you have put some effort into the beginning of this leadership model, you know where you want, and in what areas you can see the results. You may not always like or be happy with the result, but it is another story.

You know how you perform, this is also input to your feedback and improvement areas in the short and long term. Here you can also find some good why explanations for the energy / motivation block, why you practice / train something, because we can see in our results that... we need to... (Positive results continue with it, and make it even better, or negative, improvement required)

This section is about following up the process and measuring results. How can you see that you are on the right path? How can you follow the results in the short and long term? How do you see results, in areas that are not so easy to measure, where the results are not shown on the "board"?

Take care of the results

Usually we only see the hard results, your points from the hockey games, and your position in the league and so on. Many times we forget to see the progress and the results in the "soft" parts, such as working together (teamwork), better communication, improved feedback between teammates, team spirit, attitude, etc. The majority of the coaches are judged solely on results and in many cases at instant success, rather than the level of performance.

Although it is the hard results that are counted in hockey and all sports for that matter, the soft results will make sure the right pre-conditions are in place, for the hard results!

The bigger the dream, the more important the team is. A leader never gets more results than the team will deliver.

"My story as a leader cannot be compared to Frank Rijkaard's story. He has zero trophies and I have many of them ..." / Mourinho

Become a champion in 20% of your activities

I have previously mentioned the 20-80 rule in short, if you remember? Have you heard of the Pareto 20/80 rule in any context?

The Pareto rule states that 80% of your results come from 20% of your activities, exercises, routines etc. This means that a limited amount of activities already gives you 80% of the results!

Therefore, it is important to have those basic principles in place. What are your cornerstones? Or if we look at your hockey player's key or basic skills, which ones already gives you 80% of the results?

Find and visualize the important activities, drills and methods that generate the most results and get really good at doing those few things! Getting your basic frame in place makes it easier for you and your players to do things outside the box / box. Become a master of what lies within the framework and which gives you 80% of the results, then you also become good at what lies outside, but have the security in the basic activities.

Mourinho's 36 exercises

José Mourinho uses 36 basic methods or exercises. You will probably not find them, at least I have not done so, but it can give us some guidelines that he is working on the 20/80 rule?

These are some things that you can read about Mourinho's 36 exercises.

Combined exercises

The 36 exercises are simple or basic if you prefer that word, the methods are mainly designed to work with technical skills. During the training sessions and exercises, the players work combined with "fitness", tactical, technical steps and problem solving, Mourinho has also included the psychological and mental factors in the exercises, which means that he also works with the psychological part of the football to achieve the results that he has set up in the direction block.

Results
- Goal scoring

Hockey is always fair - most goals win!

Actually, goal scoring can be seen as a capacity that is trained up, but I have chosen to put that part here in results because...

The team scoring the most goals wins, it's not a secret. Several people may sometimes think that a victory has been unfair, let that statement stand for them.

In hockey goals are counted and the team that scores the most goals wins, therefore goal-scoring is important!

Match-like exercises that are completed are the key. It is also important to try to get the players to "push" themselves in every situation, we are focused when we carry out the exercise and need score goals every time (mindset).

Below are some easy to remember points for goal scoring:

1. Shoot to score a goal every time - There are no warm-up shots or "it is just training" thinking, as we train, we perform during the match and thus, equal to the results we will get.

The goalkeepers are warmed up, just as well as the players when we go out on the ice.

2. Always go towards goal - Take the rebound, the stick always on the ice, finish the situation. 90% of all goals come in the situation right after the first shot, therefore always practice on that situation in your hockey drills.

3. Play to the end - Puck in goal, blocked or passed away.

4. Freeze the goalkeeper or create side movement - Shot or pass fakes get the goalkeeper "to freeze" in the first position, sideways movement and shot, or sideways pass and finish, and you have increased your chances of scoring significantly.

Other good areas to consider are using screeners and rebound takers to as many drills as possible and if there are defenseman in the exercise, these play the puck out of zone or to the next player in the lead.

The goals are counted – Shooting skills

To win matches you need to create goal chances and use them, you have to score goals. The target for the shooter is the goal, during a regular training a player shoots about 20-30 shots, some of these will miss the target. It goes without saying that, with this number of repetitions, you do not

become a shooting master.

It takes "a little bit" more, a little more practice for example beside the ice, a number mentioned many times is 100 shots a day and then not only to feed on, but preferably shot from different positions, the puck near the body, alongside, lateral movement, etc. 100 shots, corresponds to the amount of shots from 3-4 on ice practices, it gives results, and will not take that much time to perform.

How many goals have not been scored like this?

About 90% of the goals in the NHL are made from similar situations just in front of the goal and the goalkeeper.

Look at the situation, heading forwards towards the distant rebound surface, the body / chest facing the target, both skates on the ice with good balance, the stick on the ice, ready to shoot, bent knees, low center of gravity, pass or shot from the teammate, the upper arm elbow detached from the body, gaze up, powerful and quick shot, continue toward the goal, the puck in goal ... hands up in the ceiling.

Offensive game and goal scoring

From the offensive game you can identify four main chances for goal scoring, I will describe these more closely.
 The scoring situations that we should look at are,

- Straight attack from the "slot"

- Break in from the corner / board

- Diagonal pass

- Shot from the blue line

Other scoring chances are, shot at diagonal movement, shot at deep-pass, shot at screen, rebound shot and a loose puck.

Shooting in hockey

Go straight to the goal, no turns, get a shot at goal.

A hard, fast, well-directed and unexpected shot is perhaps the optimal shot? To get to that "target picture", as always training is required. An excellent opportunity is to train at home from a shooting pad, before training on a shot ramp, but of course also to spend time and focus on the hockey training on the technique.

If we take the on ice training, it is about making the training moments as match-like as possible, in order to be able to train on goal scoring in the right environment and with the right conditions (higher stress level). Complete all situations (take rebounds) and play to the end, until the puck is dead i.e. in goal, blocked or played away from the goal.

Some keys in goal scoring are also to consider goal scoring from goalkeeper view. How do the goalkeepers not want the shots to come? Where do the goalie not want the shots? From which distance do the goalkeepers not want the shots to come? How do they not want the situation right after the shot?

"Guys shoot a lot! The other team also has a poor goalkeeper"/ Lasse Falk

"You miss 100% of the shots you don't take" / Wayne Gretzky

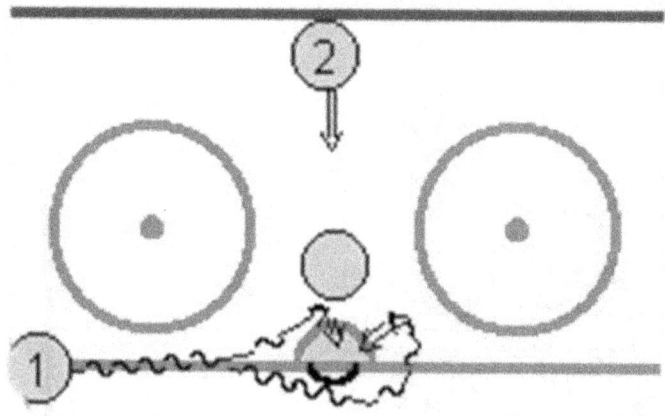

Break in from the corner at the first post or around the goal, remain as a screener in front of the goalkeeper for shot from player 2.

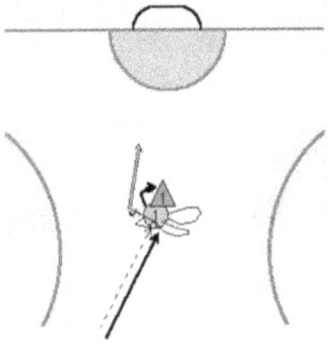

Forward 1 and defender 1 move in front of goal, forward 1 gets pass from the lead on blue and finishes quickly, defender 1 marks his presence, forward 1 becomes defender 1 and the one who has passed becomes forward 1.

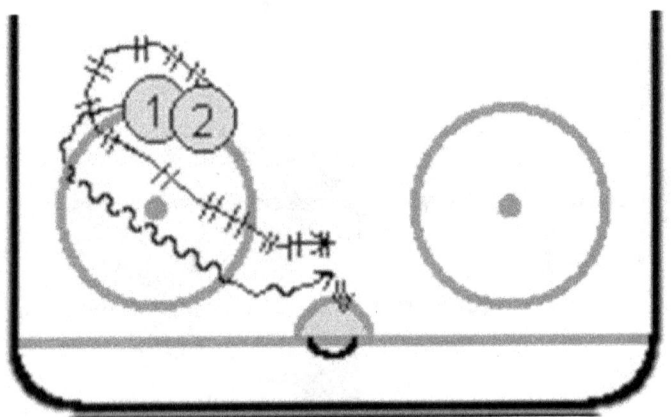

Player 1 starts with puck and breaks into goal, player 2 marks his presence.

Goal scoring - Straight attack against goals (with pass opportunity)

The puck driver goes straight to the goal and strives to shoot quickly and surprisingly, at the same time as the passing opportunity is available. If the goalkeeper reacts to the pass option, prematurely or due to pass fake, the surface opens high up at the first post (like in the picture).

The second alternative is to shoot low at the far post if the goalkeeper covers the first post. This shot also opens up for rebound shot for player two.

The role of the puck driver in both situations is to drive with speed towards the goal, timing from the other player, with the hockey stick on the ice and be prepared to shoot directly on the pass or a rebound.

Some quick drills to practice above situation, instead for long skating routes, we use a short distance towards the goal to maximize the number of repetitions.

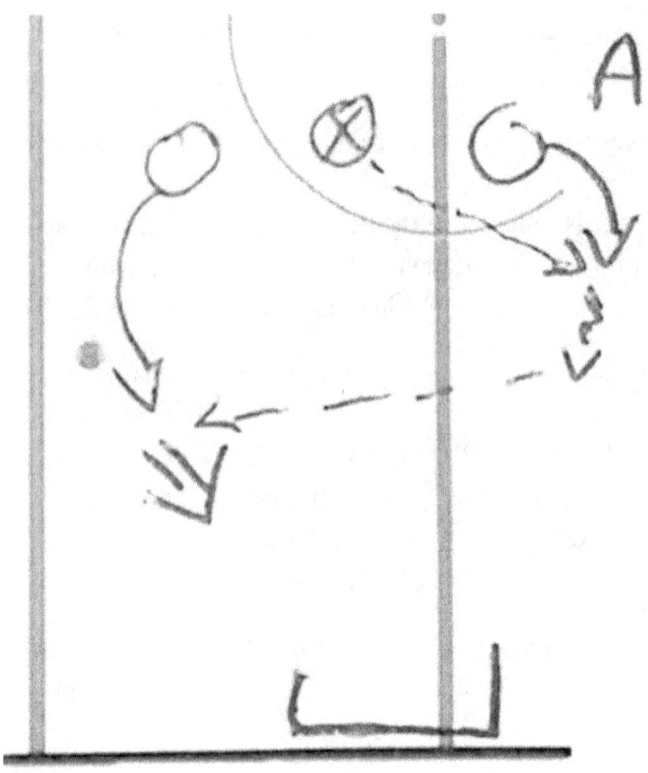

Start with three quick strides. Pass from the coach / player, 2 towards the goalkeeper. Shot or pass, take any rebound.

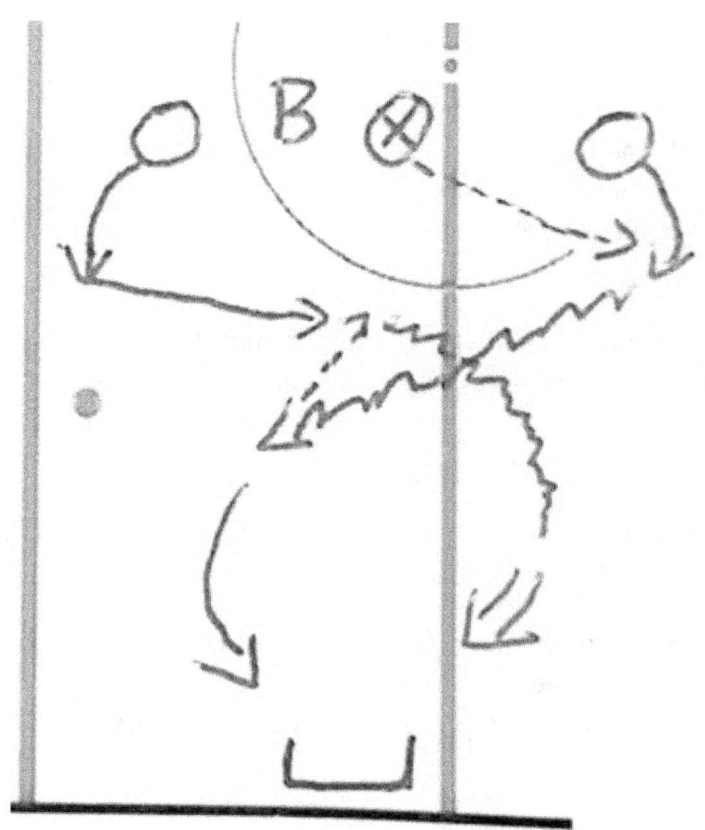

Same as above, but with change of sides / position.

Goal Scoring – Break in from Corner

The puck driver breaks in towards goal and strives to shoot quickly and surprisingly, while at the same time there is the opportunity to pass. If the goalkeeper reacts to the pass option, prematurely or due to pass fake, the surface opens high up at the first post.

If the goalkeeper is left at the post, it is important to bring the goalkeeper in a sideways movement, then open the door between the legs, high up at the glove side or after the ice at the far post.

If you shoot low, a rebound option arises if the goalkeeper saves.

The role of the puck driver in both situations is to drive with speed towards goal, timing with the other player, with the stick on the ice and be prepared to shoot directly on the pass or a rebound.

Goal Scoring - Diagonal Pass

The puck driver goes towards the goal and shows the goalkeeper that he is ready to shoot anytime, so that the goalkeeper cannot prepare for a side shift.

The pass that comes will be quick, surprising and hard. The receiver is prepared in deep position and shoots a direct shot, high in the nearest corner or low in the corner the pass and the goalkeeper comes from.

The passers role in the situation is to continue driving with speed towards the goal, with the stick on the ice, gaze at the puck and be prepared to shoot directly on the pass or a rebound.

Goal Scoring - Shot from the blue line

The puck driver at blue has a look up and knows where the nearest opponent is who can hinder the shot. Before the shot the player tries to get the goalkeeper in lateral movement, then a quick shot.

The non-puck driver creates a screen in front of the goalkeeper, which can happen both near the goalkeeper, but also higher up on the surface. The screening player is prepared both for steering and rebounds.

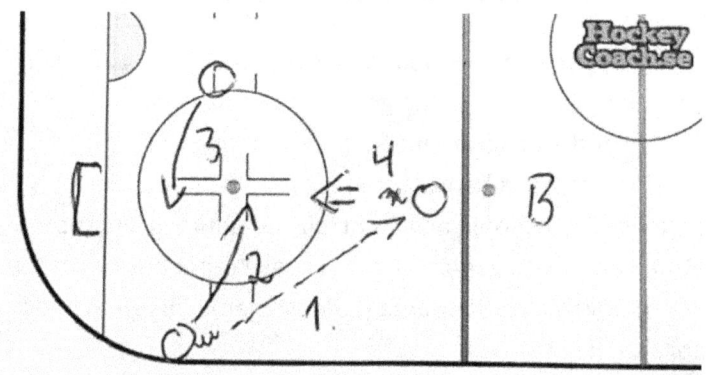

Hockey drill B 1. Pass up to blue 2. Enter the upper screening zone 3. Enter the lower screening zone 4. Shot from blue. Play the situation to the end.

If there are no own screening players, the player on the blue line can try to use the opponents by moving the puck so that the shot is screened by the opponents' players for the goalkeeper.

The puck sees the target chances with other eyes

The goalkeepers always strive to place themselves in the central line of the puck. Therefore, it is also important for the players to be able to "see" or imagine the goal scoring situation from the point of view of the puck. The puck and the player do not see the same things and openings in the goal.

Through fast sideways movements and a quick shot, the shooter can gain an advantage.

After the shot - The rebound area and the rebound

In order to access the rebound, desire is required, it is tough and crowded in front of the goal, but it is also where the majority of the goals are made, poking, lifting or a new shot. Therefore, create a habit of training that in all situations on the drills, these should always be played until the situation is finished and that everyone works to take rebounds or get the puck removed from that area (defenseman). This gives good habits to the matches.

After a first shot you can also, for example, have a 1 against 1 battle situation where the players enter the rebound.

Other important areas in goal scoring

Balance - be able to shoot in difficult and different positions

Coordination - a difficult movement with hockey stick and body before the shot

Own players who screen the goalkeeper...

Screen the goalkeeper - make it difficult for the goalkeeper to see the puck by being between the shooter and the goalkeeper or just passing in front of the goalkeeper just when the shot comes.

Goal scoring statistics

It can be fun to think about what is required to score goals from a statistical perspective. All figures are general, but with a base in reality.

1-2 shots of 10 go in, that means, if you shoot between 10-15 shots, then you should probably keep your own goal clear in order to be able to win a match. If you get away 30 shots, it could at best correspond to 6 goals scored.

9 out of 10 goals are made from the surface in front of the goal, so make sure the puck and you are in that area.

On 10 power plays, 2-4 goals are made. Stay on the ice or take advantage of the benefit.

Power play

Screen, shoot and take rebounds, three simple handy tips for a successful power play. If you take it further, this can be categorized into additional power play tips.

- Always have a screening player in front of the goalkeeper. An intersecting screener that "turns off the lamp" for the goalkeeper just at the shot moment higher up the ice, gives even better effect (look at the drill few pages ago).

- Two players ready to go on predetermined rebound areas.

- Puck tempo in passes and direct shots

- Create time through pass speed

Goal scorer's checklist

"It is difficult to become a good goal scorer, if you skate around thinking about nice passes" / Mats Sundin

As a small summary on the keys for goal scoring, I have compiled a list of reminders or checklists of important things to consider:
- The main purpose of hockey is to strive to score goals, hockey is always fair, most goals win.
- Be healthy selfish in goal scoring situations.
- Hide the shot and surprise the goalkeeper.
- Use screening players to your advantage.
- If there are no screeners, use the opponent. Move the puck before the shot so that the opponent is the one who screens your shot for his own goalkeeper.
- Force the goalkeeper to act in the middle of a movement.
- Without puck towards the goal, with the blade on the ice and good position.
- Be serious in all practices, there are no warm-up shots
- Shoot a lot, but not desperately.
- Follow skilled goal scorers on e.g. YouTube or Instagram, how do they do?
- Follow the goalkeepers' actions in different situations, in order to understand how they react.
- 90% of the goals are made from the surface directly in front of the goal, be sure to be there, be prepared.
- Play all situations to the end.

New Behaviors - New Results

Few things are as stupid as hoping that old behaviors and activities will give you new results. If you get good results, continue. If you do not get the results you want, you need to evaluate the other parts of the model, where does it fail?

- Commit yourself to being the master of what you do, is the new standard of success and good results. Be so good that people can't ignore seeing you. Nothing less than my very best in every moment!

"I intend to do my best, improve things and create cooperation in relation to my image and my philosophy." /
José Mourinho

Feedback

Leadership responsibility		Team Responsibility			
		Teamwork			
Energy / Engagement	Direction / Goals	Capacity	+ Team Spirit	- Collaboration losesses	Results (Hard and soft)
Feedback and learning					

Feedback

Leadership responsibility				Team Responsibility	
		Teamwork			
Energy / Engagement	Direction / Goals	Capacity	+ Team Spirit	- Collaboration losesses	Results (Hard and soft)
Feedback and learning					

Feedback

How was the result? How was the energy, motivation, teamwork and results? What did we do well? What can be improved? What have we learned? What do we take with us in the future? Your feedback will affect all parts of the model, the energy, direction, cooperation and the results you will achieve in the future. This is perhaps the part that many of us do not spend so much time on, or if we lack time, e.g. after an exercise it is, the block that we are likely to skip, but this is important. It is about learning for the future, for the next exercise, training, match, so that it will be good over time.

"I hate to talk to players individually. Players do not win trophies, teams win trophies ... I love players who love to win. They win not only for 90 minutes, but every day, every workout, every moment of their lives" / José Mourinho

See the possibilities - feedback and evaluation

There is a clear link between quickly getting rid of your previous negative thoughts related to your performance and your performance in the next hockey drill, practice or match.

If you have "driven off the road" into the ditch, you will meet two alternatives, stay in the ditch and complain about your situation and feel sorry for yourself.

Or you can immediately start the steps to get you back on the road again, get your focus back on the original plan (what and how) and learn something for the future, why did I end up in the ditch (did it go too fast? Lack of skills? etc.). Next time I know I have to keep my focus and stand on the brakes a little bit earlier.

It is okay to run off in a curve (make mistakes), but do not run out in the same curve twice!

Refocus

Those who are good at refocusing are able to refocus and thereby avoid unnecessary energy leakage and maintain their self-confidence better than those who get stuck in the "situation" and groan at the previous shift, for example.

Many times, players will continue to get negative thoughts after a mistake. What if I will fail again? What happens if I get hurt? What if I will not succeed?

All this can be changed to, what happens if I have fun again? What if I'm good? What happens when I succeed? Why not try again, great opportunity to make it work.

This is something you can visualize and communicate to your players and direct their thinking in the right direction. Help your players create accurate and positive images. Focus on what to do now, not on what to avoid.

"Now we should not let in more goals and we should not be nervous, just because we lead the final."

Remember the example with lemon or basketball example, think the right thoughts act right. You, the feedback and how it's delivered is the key!

Feedback is also one of the tools in follow-up dialogues. How are things progressing / going? How have you experienced the training? Development? What has worked well? What has been a challenge? How can you as a coach support? What have you seen as the leader?

 To be able to coach and support the development, we also need to understand the individual driving forces, something drives the player to come to the training, WHY?

Feedback for all players, from striker to "waterboy"

To avoid social loafing (= I'm not important, no one will see if I don't do my best, there are other players), it's important that you give feedback to all your players so they know you see them and they feel that they are unique, important and meaningful to the team's performance and success. This is especially important for the players with less "glamorous" . roles, in many cases, for example, the defensemen receive less visibility and feedback, if you are not "Erik Karlsson" in San Jose Sharks.

Pay attention to your left or right defensemen for their defensive qualities as well. The same goes for hard-working centers or in some cases box play specialists.

All players are needed in the team during the season, create a sense of it. There will be changes that you can be assured of, development, injuries etc. that will affect the team's structure and composition.

See each individual achievement

You need to ensure that you see every single achievement and can provide feedback so that players cannot get into the trap of social loafing, they should feel that you see them, all the time and thus increase the value of their performance, you show them that every player is important to the team's success.

The above is of course applicable during both hockey games and training. Watch José Mourinho during the matches, he takes notes and writes in his little notebook throughout the game. It is impossible to remember everything from the matches or the training ... Your notes will help you to give precise and correct feedback after a hockey match or exercise to each player and the message becomes stronger if you can correctly refer to the game situation.

In addition to direct feedback and feedback in other situations, team meetings and individual meetings with each player will be a good method to avoid social loafing.

Feedback Guidelines

- Do it immediately if possible, otherwise take notes and be precise when you have the opportunity.

- Be exact (use examples from the game and the performance during practice, describe and show the correct execution)

- Respond to an action or behavior (not person)

- Use "I" messages, I know ... I can see...

- Keep it short

- Use silence (silence causes the player / players to reflect and think)

- Open up for a solution, (how do you feel yourself? How can you do it differently?)

- Summarize at the end, "OK, as you said ... ... is it / can it be good, if you try to do (... sum up how ...) next time.

"Give feedback to your best players, otherwise they will not be the best in the long run, but also give feedback to the worse players so they know that you know..." / Swedish hockey coach

After each match, Mourinho thanked all his players on the pitch and on the bench. He does this by hugging them and / or touching their head, not many managers / leaders / coaches have this kind of close contact with their players.

Positive reinforcement

Basically all feedback can be given as positive reinforcement or energy-eating negative.

Avoid mistakes, or We continue with the safe game that we have right now.

Don't whine, or Communicate positive signals to each other all the time.

We must not get stuck on blue, or We quickly pass our own blue.

Do not think that it hurts or We are strong and continue, push each other.

Don't do that ... or If you do this or in this way...

When we say what we should not do, it is not always natural, what we really are expected to do, therefore it is of course better to deliver the message in the form of what we are expected to do.

Do you have any own negative comments that you can turn to something that strengthens your players and gives them the right images and thoughts? The negative "infects", but the positive part is that the positive feedback also "infects".

Hard days will always come, but run out?

What others think of you is not your "business". Leadership is about having a harmless belief in your vision, goals and your power to do positive things with your hockey team, this does not mean that you do not listen to others or the feedback you receive, hard days will always come, but does not mean that you need to change something immediately.

It is also the belief in success and the belief that you should continue, in the direction you have set out, that allows you to give correct feedback back to the team, to provide more energy and keep a clear direction.

If you give up your "foundation stones" or vision, it will be difficult for you to see and understand what gives results and not, you are no longer you. In case of changes in the leadership style, you need to change a little at a time and systematically if this is necessary. The same goes for the game, trying to find the right changes from the foundation stones, not always by replacing them.

Remember that hard days always come, but never last forever, but strong people do. Hard times are just opportunities to learn for the future!

Hard times build good leaders and hockey players. During the difficult times and pressure your leadership ability and skills are tested. You can't always control everything, things will happen, learn how to handle them.

"If everything is under control, you run too slowly" / Mario Andretti, racing driver

"The only thing we can't control is our supporters" / José Mourinho

"Pain is temporary. Giving up lasts forever". / Lance Armstrong

"Big leaders and teams create castles of the stones that others throw at them, but it is impossible to build a castle of excuses."

Celebrate with the team or with me?

If you listen to some interviews after matches and depending on the results, you will probably hear a difference. Many times, negative results or performance is explained by external factors (bad luck with referees calls, unlycky, it was a little bit "post out" today, poor preparation due to late flight / bus delay, etc.), or weak internal factors we tried, but today we failed to live up to our ability.

The success, on the other hand, is most likely described with the own team's internal strength and successful ways to pick up opportunities and skills in crucial situations or the success of an individual team member, which is probably quite precise and detailed. Do you recognize it?

"The line referee scored goals. Nobody knows if that shot went over the goal line and you have to be 100% sure when you say it's goal" / José Mourinho

If you provide feedback or explain the team's performance, the following aspects should be considered.

Control - Control of the situation, who was responsible. Teams / players who explain their failures or successes with external causes, such as "one timers", where there is no control for the team / player are likely to end up in a bad negative trend.

On the other hand, when teams / players explain the success of internal cause (own effort, skills, etc.), stability over time (we / I can and will be able to do it again) and we did so because we acted according to "game plan" or as we have practiced (control), get better chances to perform well next time too.

Here, as a coach, you have an important role to play, when you explain the results (cause, stability and control) will also affect the degree of how much your team members will explain the results in this way and how they play during the match. The same principle can be applied to feedback on events during a hockey match.

Feedback during the hockey game

Your feedback during a match can usually be divided into three categories:
- Positive or negative reinforcement
- Technical instructions
- General encouragement
How do you "play" your coaching role during a match?

"99% of the feedback from the coaches is to players when they have the puck. Ironically, hockey players only have the puck on their stick in 0.2% of the hockey game."

"In half-time, Mourinho told me that" I want more intensity from your side, you are not the Milito I know, and you just walk around at the pitch"- After that I scored two goals." /
Diego Milito

How about the feedback between players during a match? If you look at the celebration after a goal, how does the scorer act? Going away from the team, or to the teammates? Was it his or her goal, or the team's goal?

Feedback to the team or individuals?

There may also be differences in whether you talk about teams or individuals when you explain or give feedback on the result. Should you strengthen the team or the individuals in the team?

In teams with low team spirit or in a losing team, it tends to be a more individual aspect to explain the results (there are some players who do not reach their usual level, individual mistakes made etc.) and in teams with good team spirit and communication within the team, the team aspect is more common, both when it comes to victories, as losses, we win as a team, we lose as a team. This part is quite interesting to have in mind when listening to interviews after a game, what is said tells you something about the team spirit.

Make a mistake to a complete mistake

Finally, a sentence about the most common cause of feedback from the coach or teammates, mistakes. This is the most common feedback we provide in various forms, it's linked to a mistake (negative feedback or general encouragement, "come on")

Does it really make any difference, to reinforce the mistake with further communication about it?

The same applies to the players' reaction after a mistake and the feedback to themselves...

"Everyone makes mistakes, but to get upset and show it, make the mistake complete"
(Look! It was me who did it!!!!!)

Check out this reaction after a mistake from defenseman nr 2
http://youtu.be/92tnSvzk7t8

There is some truth in what you say

If you get criticism or negative feedback, instead of protecting yourself with excuses or explanations, try to say to yourself, "There is some truth in what you say, and there's a reason why you say it". Take the feedback with you and value it later ... there was some truth and reason behind???

Set the communication frequency

When you talk about feedback you can also talk about senders and receivers here, as we talked about earlier connected to communication and if it was only about these two roles, it would be easy to give feedback. But feedback takes time and has more aspects to consider, you have the skills, experience, expectations and environment that can affect your feedback.

If you have great expertise and experience in a subject, it will probably affect how you express yourself and depending on the recipient's competence and experience, your message will be interpreted in different ways. The recipient will also be affected by his / her feelings for the moment, expectations of your feedback and the recipient can therefore sometimes also turn off in certain situations, because he / she knows what is coming...

The environment will of course also affect your feedback, during a match it can be "noise" from the audience / parents who will interfere with the feedback (you give feedback about puck possession and parents shouting for shots). If / when it is possible to provide feedback after the match, you can choose an environment where you can give your feedback in a good way and you know that the other person is at least not disturbed by the environment.

Are you with, do you understand? Yes...

A little repetition of the past, but it fits in so well even on the feedback section...

When you give feedback to your players keep track of whether they are listening, are they present? Do they watch you, nod or shake their heads, cross arms (not receptive)?

It can be difficult to check if your players have understood your feedback if you do as most of us do, by asking, do you understand? And the answer is, yes!

What if you only asked the player (in the case of individual feedback) or one of the players (team feedback) to briefly summarize what you have said, so that everyone has the same image of the feedback, and you would get a receipt of understanding?

When the feedback has been repeated you can ask if they think this is the way to do it next time? Or if they have their own views, involvement creates energy (which may need to be targeted...)

I can't hear you, my ego wants attention

In order to give and listen to feedback, you need to understand the other person's perspective, and this can be difficult if you have a different opinion or are anxious to express your feedback, comment or reply, but there is a good rule, you have to release your own perspective in order to be able to understand someone else, actually what feedback is about and the meaning of it. Listen, reflect, ask and embrace (or in some cases throw away, after reflection).

In practice, this means that you cannot take the feedback the other person gives you if you think of your own feedback, comment or how to respond to the feedback, if you do not release your own perspective, and this applies to all of us.

Remember the guideline, there is some truth in what you say, and there is a reason behind it, why you say it.

"Many have such great egos screaming so loudly that they can't hear what the other says"

Summary

Leadership responsibility			Teamwork			Team Responsibility
Energy / Engagement	Direction / Goals	Capacity	+ Team Spirit	- Collaboration losesses	Results (Hard and soft)
		Feedback and learning				

Hare and turtle

Finally, a well-known story about the hare and the turtle, which can somehow summarize many of the aspects of learning in this book and the leadership model.

The turtle and the hare argued about who was the fastest. They decided to solve the "trouble" with a competition. They agreed on a route and started the race. The hare started quickly and ran fast for some time. Soon he realized that he was far before the turtle and that he could relax under a tree for a while before continuing the competition.

The hare lay under the tree and fell asleep soon. The turtle picked meters by meter on him with small steps and soon took over the lead and could even cross the finish line as the undisputed champion.

The hare woke up and realized that he had lost the race. The story's morality is that slow and steady wins the competition. This is the version of the story that we have all grown up with. But recently I heard a more interesting version of this story. It continues...

The hare and the turtle had become quite good friends at this time and they thought a little about each other. Both realized that the last race could have been carried out in a much better way.

If the hare had not taken things as obvious, then the turtle had not beaten him. So he challenged the turtle to a new race. The turtle accepted the challenge.

This time, the hare went out and ran without stopping, from start to finish. He won with several kilometers.

The moral of the story?

Fast and consistent will always beat slow and stable.
If you have two people in your organization or your team, a slow, methodical, and reliable, and the other quick and reliable on what he does, the fast and reliable will consistently climb the organizational steps faster than the slow methodical.

It is good to be slow and stable; but it is better to be quick and reliable.

But the story doesn't end here.
The turtle thought a little, and realized that there was no way that he could beat the hare in a competition in this format. He thought for a while and then challenged the hare to another competition, but on a slightly different route.

Hare accepted and the competition started. In line with his own conviction and commitment to being consistently quick, he took off and ran at the highest speed until he came to a wide river.

The finish line was a few kilometers across the river.
The hare was sitting there thinking about what to do.
Meanwhile, the turtle has arrived at the river, swam over, and
continued over the finish line.

The moral of the story?

First, identify your core competency and then change the
playing field to suit your core competency.
If you are a good speaker, make sure you create opportunities
to give presentations, which make it possible to exploit that
strength.
If analyzes are your strength, make sure that you use it in the
form of different analyzes of opponents, your own players,
game systems etc. Working with your strengths will not only
make you appear, but also create opportunities for
development and progress.

The story has still not ended.

The hare and the turtle were now even closer friends at this
time and they thought a little about each other. Both realized
that the last race could have been done much better.
So they decided to run the last race again, but running like a
team this time.
They started, and this time, the hare was carrying the turtle
to the water. There the turtle took over and swam with the
hare on his back.

On the opposite beach, the hare again carried the turtle and they reached the finish line together. They both felt a greater sense of satisfaction than they had known before.

The moral of the story?

It is good to be individually brilliant and have strong core competencies, but if you cannot work in a team and utilize each other's core competencies, you will always perform "under par" (golf term) because there will always be situations where you perform worse and someone else is doing well.

The collaboration is mainly about situational leadership, which means that the person with relevant core competence for a situation, takes the leadership right there.

There are more lessons learned from this story. Note that neither the hare nor the turtle gave up after failures. The hare decided to work harder and make more effort after his failure.

The turtle changed his strategy because he was already working as hard as possible.
IRL (In Real Life), when we face a failure, it is sometimes appropriate to work harder and make more effort. Sometimes it is advisable to change strategy and try something else. And sometimes it is advisable to do both.

The hare and the turtle also learned something else important. When we stop competing against a rival (sometimes within our own team) and instead start competing against the situation, we perform much better.

So the important lessons are:
- The fast and consistent will always beat the slow and consistent
- Motivation beats class
- Work with your skills / core competencies (capacity)
- Working as a team against a common goal will always beat individual "stars" (teamwork and team spirit)
- Never give up when you face adversity
- Compete against the situation. Not against a rival (see your own performance)
- Take care of the lessons (feedback)

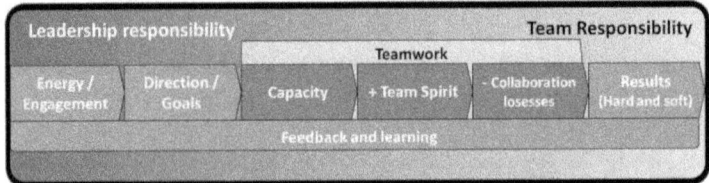

Finally, I want to thank you for reading this book. I really hope I could wake some thoughts and give you some new valuable insights. If you are interested in another book, you will find more hockey drill focus and individual skill development in this book:

Search by title or author name to find it in a bookstore or visit Hockeycoach.se.

Empty practice plans for notes

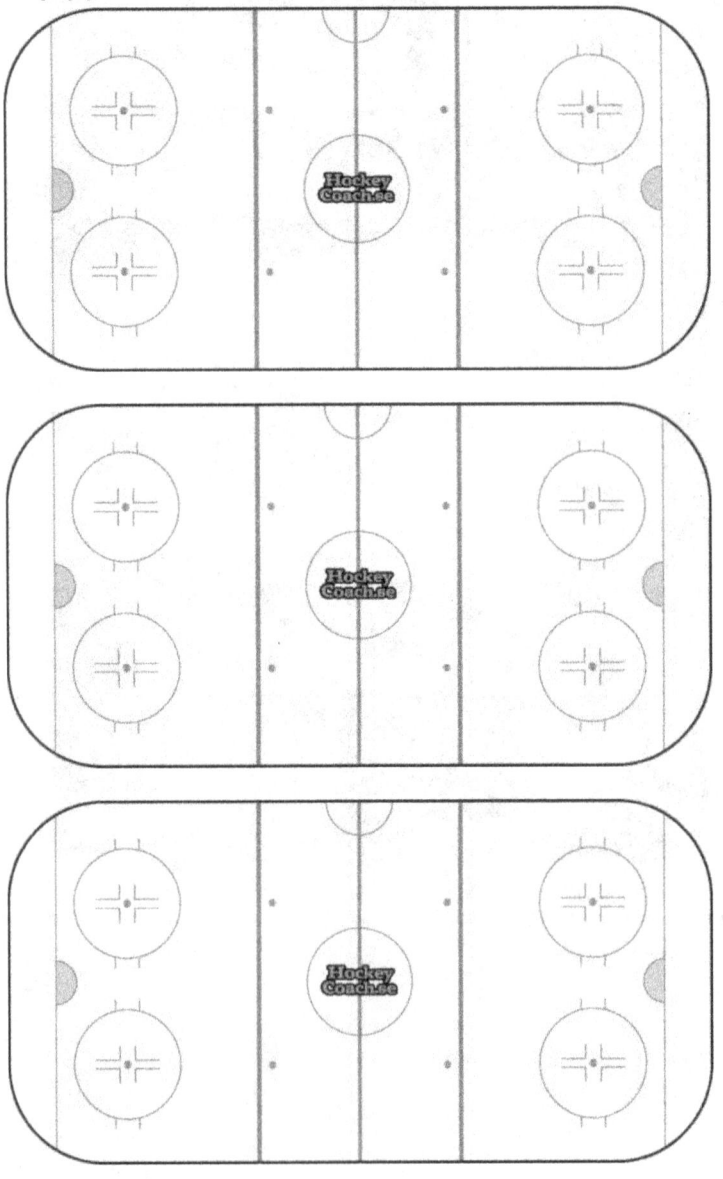

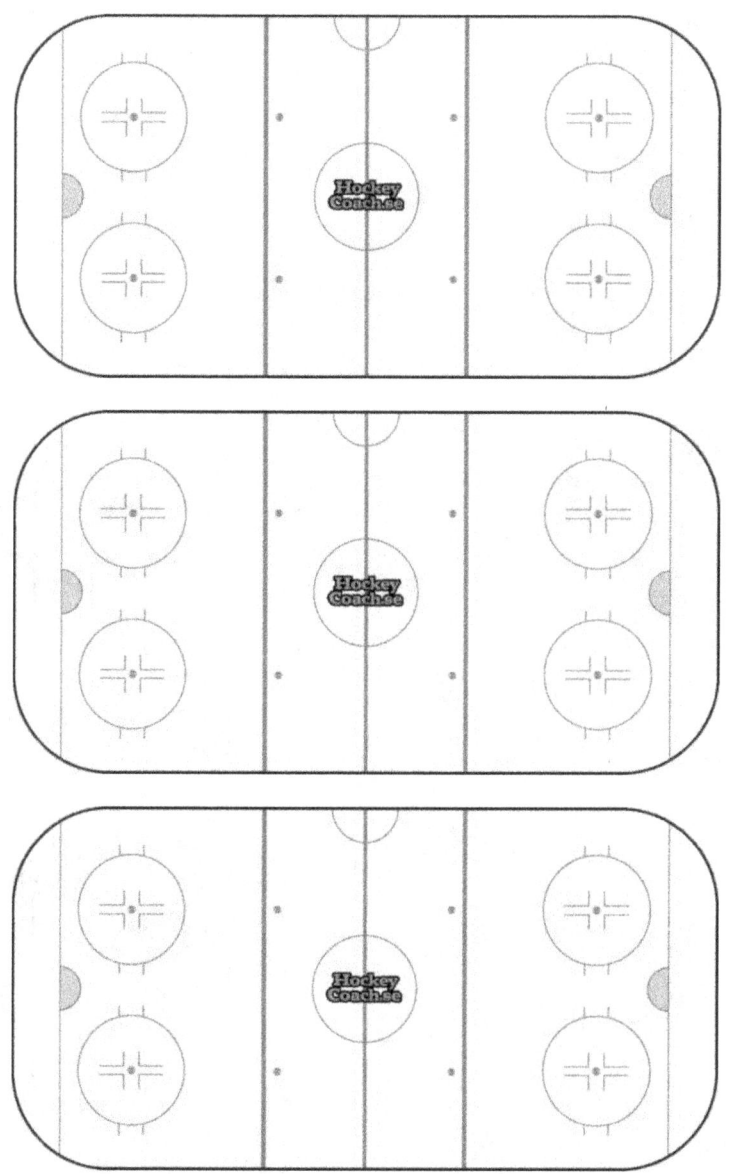

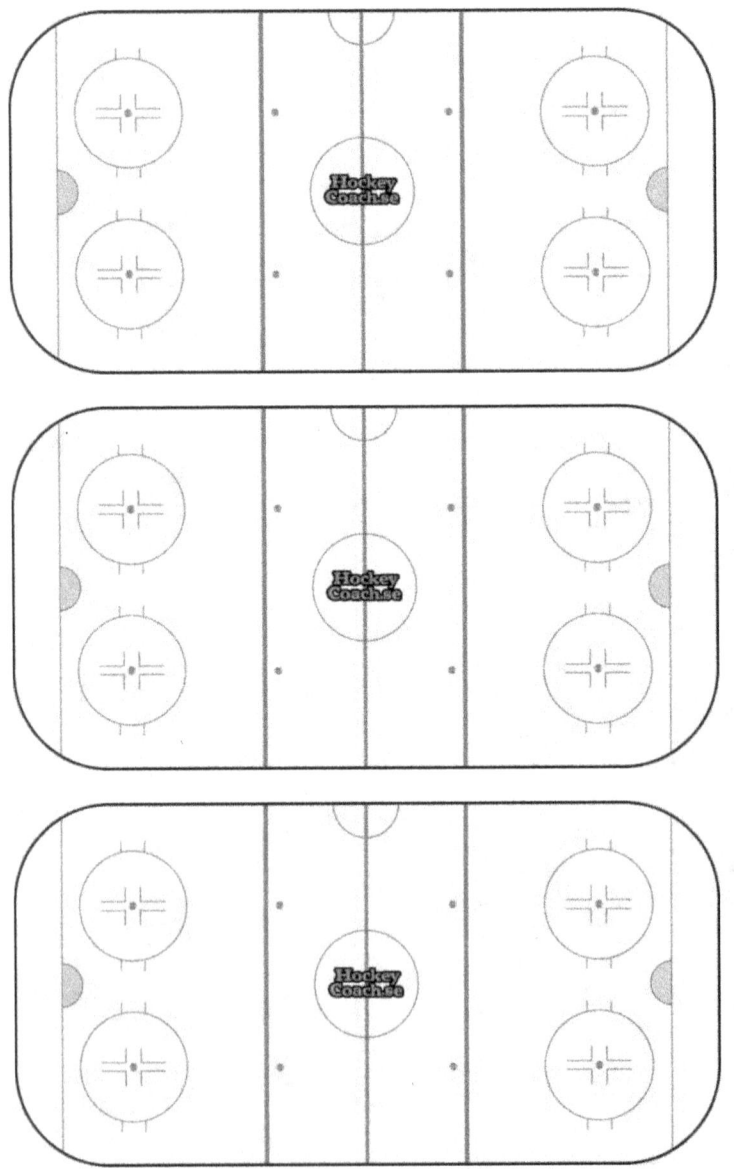

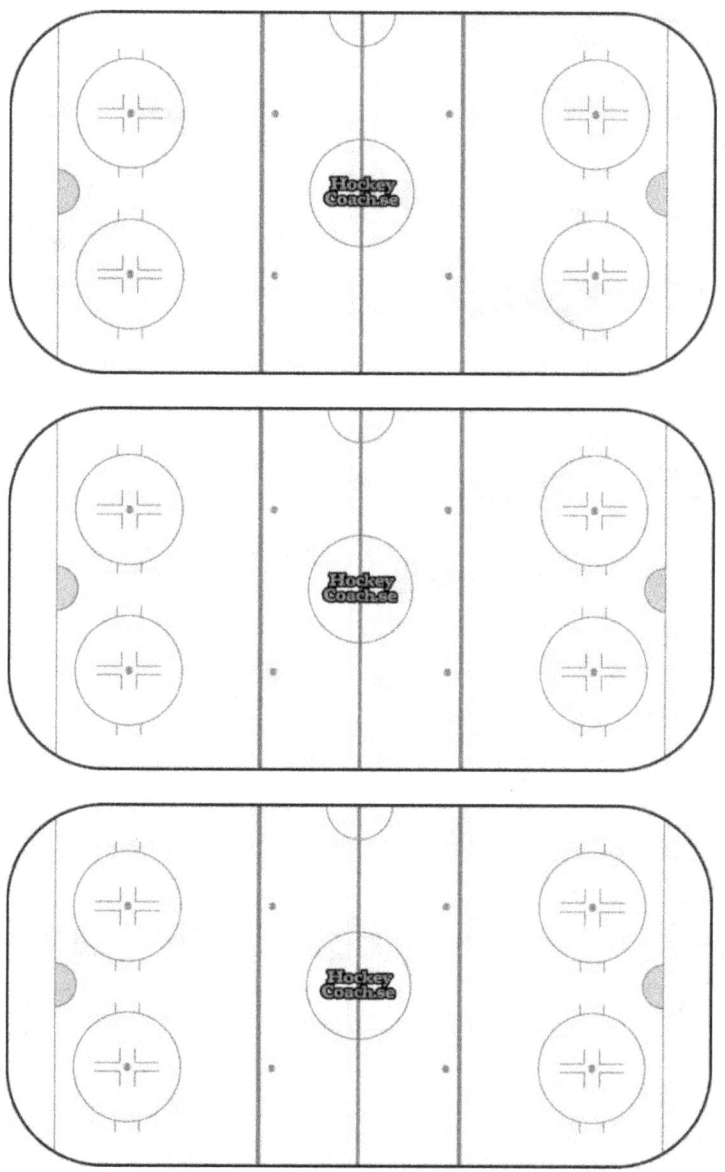

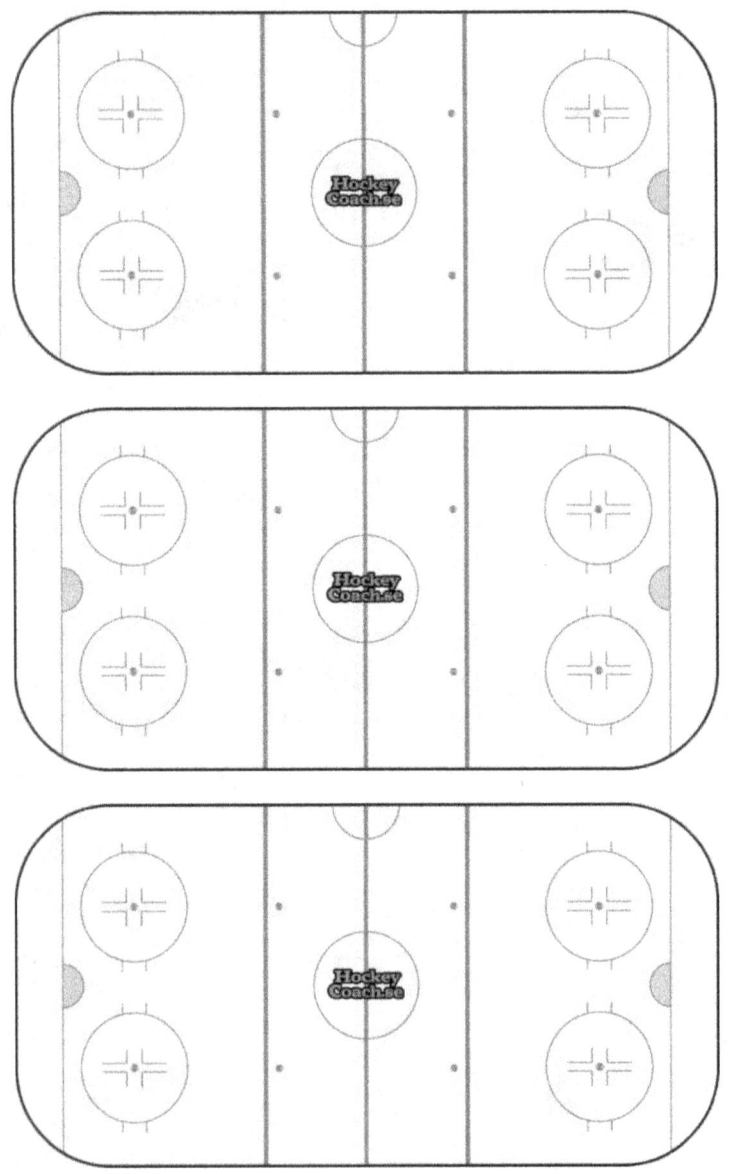

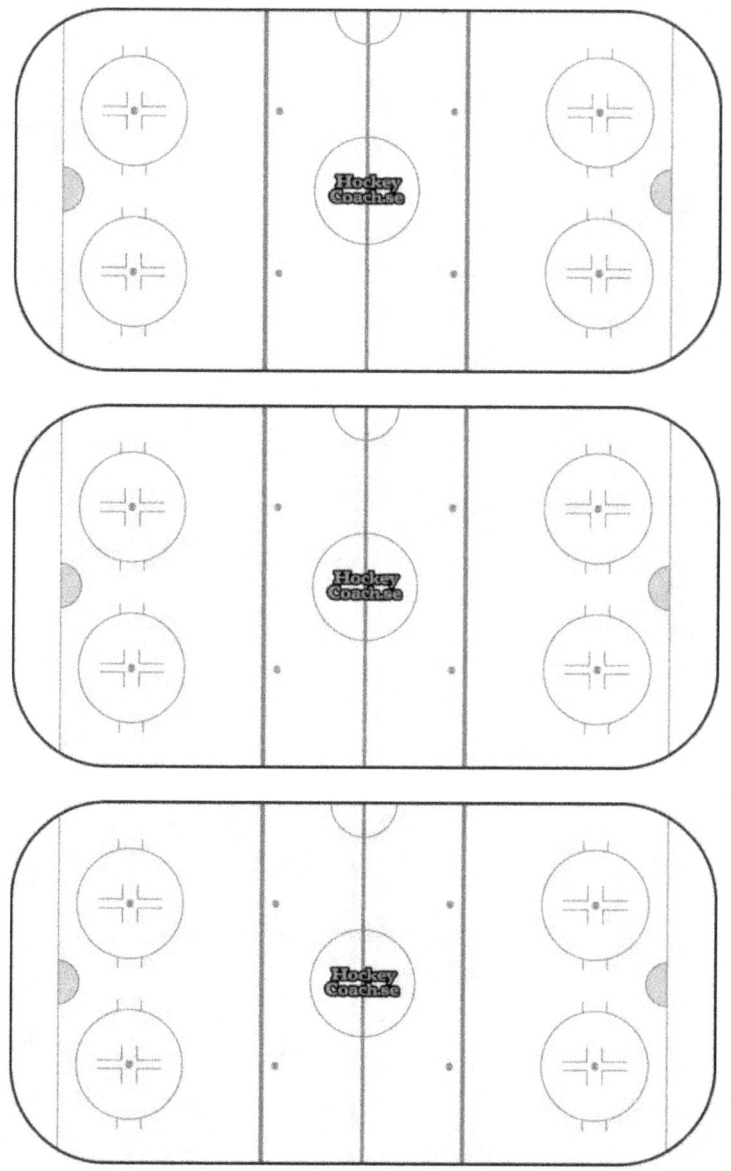

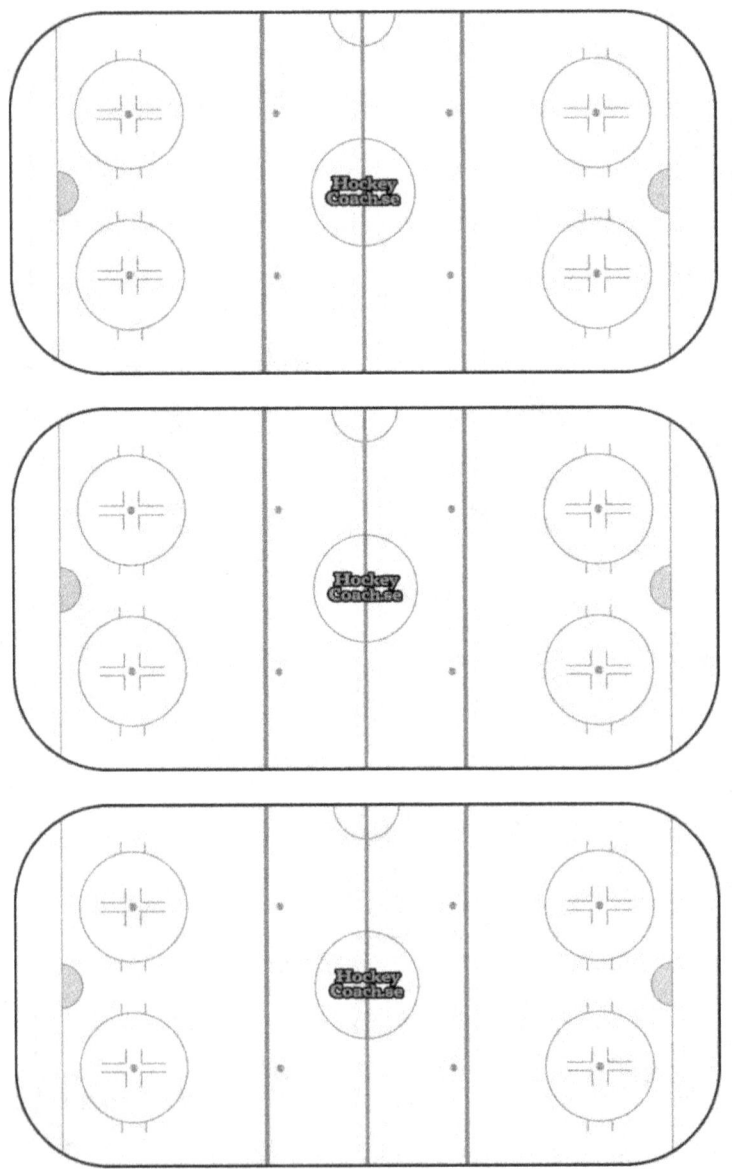

Notes

Finally I would like to thank my family for the understanding approach to all my "hockey related projects" like this book and other books and the time I spend on the ice, you are the best!

To my children Ville, Atte and Emmi, maybe you will also read this book one day, and find these rows on the last page, you are and will always be my big inspiration, energy and direction in life ☺

CPSIA information can be obtained
at www.ICGtesting.com
Printed in the USA
LVHW020856080921
697193LV00012B/1055